BROOKFIELD FREE PUBLIC LIBRARY

3 0056 00119 0848

W9-BPM-506

What's Food Got To Do With It?

101 Natural Remedies for Learning Disabilities

BROOKFIELD FREE PUBLIC LIBRARY
3609 GRAND BLVD.
BROOKFIELD, IL 60513

Sandra Hills, N.D.
Pat Wyman, M.A.

The Center for New Discoveries In Learning
Windsor, California

Printed in the United States of America. Brief quotations may be included in a review with attribution. Otherwise, no part of this book may be reproduced or transmitted in any form or by any means, electronically or otherwise, including photocopying, recording, e-mail or Internet, or by any information storage and retrieval system; sent, sold or delivered by any electronic or printed means without the express written permission of the authors. To do so constitutes a violation of the Federal copyright laws. For information, send requests to:

The Center for New Discoveries in Learning
Post Office Box 1019
Windsor, California 95492-1019   U.S.A.

Important!   The information in this book is presented to enhance your knowledge; it is not intended as a substitute for medical evaluation and treatment by a licensed physician. While every care has been taken to ensure the accuracy of the content, the authors and the publisher expressly disclaim any legal responsibility arising out of experimentation with the methods described. Any recommendations should be followed only with the advice and under the supervision of your physician or health care professional.

ISBN: 1-890047-24-4 Library of Congress Catalog: 96-092935

Copyright © 1997 - by Sandra Hills and Pat Wyman
Copyright © 1997 - Illustrations by Levi Miller
All Rights Reserved

*We lovingly dedicate this book to every child
born with the unique gift of learning
in a special way.*

*May we soon teach ourselves to treasure these
precious gifts without the need for labels.*

About the Authors

Sandra Hills,, N.D., is a Naturopathic Doctor and the founder of the American Nutrition Society for Northern California. She is also the co-author of *An Outline to Nutrition and Smart Foods, Smart Kids, Eat Your Way to Greater Brain Power*. She received her Naturopathic Doctor degree from the Anglo American Institute of Drugless Therapy in Scotland/England and is a member of the British Guild of Drugless Therapy in England. She has been an Instructor of Nutrition at Whole Life University in San Francisco and presently teaches adult education courses. She has researched the relationship between learning disabilities and nutrition for over 20 years and is a nationally recognized lecturer and researcher. Dr. Hills had her own television program in Contra Costa County on nutrition and has frequently appeared on radio and television programs related to nutrition.

Pat Wyman, M.A. is an Adjunct Instructor of Education at California State University, Hayward, Extension Division. She is also the Director of The Center for New Discoveries in Learning, a non-profit organization which disseminates educational products and information for teachers, children and parents. She trains teachers nationwide and has collected data from over 40,000 students whose grades were raised to "A's" and "B's" after using the learning strategies from her "Super Teaching Strategies" trainings and video courses. Ms. Wyman is also co-author of *Smart Foods, Smart Kids, Eat Your Way to Greater Brain Power* and author of *School Smart Kids Newsletter*. She has studied the effect of nutrition on learning for the past several years and has frequently contributed newspaper and magazine articles, radio and TV interviews about learning styles and learning how to learn. For more information about how to help your child be more successful in school please visit The Center for New Discoveries in Learning award-winning website at http://www.discoveries.org.

Table of Contents

Table of Contents

Acknowledgments

Our families have given us the time and love we needed to complete our mission and we especially thank them here: Joe Wyman, Erin and J.P. Mavredakis, Tanya Hills, Russell and Elizabeth Martino, Teri and Jim Webb. They devoted endless hours to editing, encouraging, making suggestions, and just plain listening when we needed it most.

We also want to thank our special friends who have read countless rewrites and continued to patiently read and offer comments and significant editing help. We thank Tina Maffia, Stephen Guffanti, M.D., William Crook, M.D., Beth Gilman, O.D., Greg Gilman O.D., Andrea Davis, Liz Maddox, Molly Landwehr and Teri Webb.

We also want to thank our pioneer teachers: William Crook, M.D, William Philpott M.D., Jeffrey Bland, Ph.D., and Adele Davis.

We offer a most special tribute to a remarkable 17 year old who illustrated our book and designed the cover art. Levi Miller is a great artist and a shining star. His talents are legendary at his high school and in his town. His sketches, comic books and paintings are precious gifts to his many friends. He read our book with great caring and love and devoted many hours to making pictures of our words.

A very special thanks goes to Liz Vaughn who created the production artwork for the cover.

We offer our deepest gratitude for the support and friendship of Ms. Elinor Scott and Mr. Sam Graci.

Prologue

Our children are so precious to us that whenever they struggle, we feel their pain. A child given a label to wear, takes it on, and begins to think that it must be true. But in our hearts, we know that every child is a beautiful, perfect, and a wondrous being -- and no label, learning disabled or otherwise is who any child really is.

This book is only a beginning - think of it as a new start to give your child every possible advantage as he or she is growing up.

One of the best ways to help your child is to give the gift of health and wellness. Health will last a lifetime and see your child through every challenge and every reward that life has to offer.

In our fast lane lives, sometimes our children eat foods that are not nourishing and perhaps even harmful. Although you may not be aware now of the connection between food and your child's health, behavior and ability to learn, these pages will serve as your guide to a new beginning - one to see your child through a lifetime of new learnings and radiant health.

Introduction

Each year, thousands more children are added to the ever-growing list of "learning disabled" children. In addition, current statistics reveal that over 5% of school children (about 3.5 million) have received the newest, most talked about *problem-child* label -- Attention, Deficit Hyperactivity Disorder (ADHD). What is even more startling: millions of these children are prescribed mind-altering, stimulant drugs like Ritalin or Dexedrine as a panacea for behavior problems or to help them "learn."

Sadly, studies on the ability of these drugs to truly increase learning, tell us that academic improvement is often short lived. Although students become more compliant and follow the rules better, many also suffer from serious side effects and the challenge of drug abuse issues.

We believe that no human being, in the name of behavior and learning, should have to endure the kind of side effects parents, teachers and physicians have observed repeatedly in children taking these drugs. Many children become robotic, spacey, listless, anxious and emotionless. They often lose their appetite, lose too much weight, develop nausea, stomach aches, headaches, facial tics, insomnia and depressive states. Some children even become suicidal. A major authoritative listing on all drugs, *The Physicians Desk Reference,* lists more than 25 adverse reactions from the use of Ritalin.

In addition to the side effects, another big danger is the abuse potential of these drugs. Comments made by a Drug Enforcement Administration (DEA) representative during the Conference of "Stimulant Use In The Treatment of ADHD" in

San Antonio, Texas in December, 1996, shows "that there has been a 1,000% increase in drug abuse injury reports involving methylphenidate (Ritalin) for children in the 10-14 year age group. This now equals or exceeds reports for the same age group involving cocaine.

Of further note, is the fact that the DEA lists Ritalin and Dexedrine as Schedule II drugs. Drugs are scheduled into five classes based on their abuse potential. Schedule I drugs are heroin and LSD. Ritalin and Dexedrine are in the same classification as opium and morphine, both addictive drugs. Many newspaper headlines and television news shows are calling attention to the fact that children without prescriptions, are actually stealing these stimulant drugs from school medicine cabinets, just for the induced high they get from their use.

What's more, in 1996, the manufacturer of Ritalin, Ciba Geigy Corporation, mailed over 100,000 warning letters to physicians who prescribe Ritalin. The letters notified them of the results of a study by the National Toxicology Program in which mice developed elevated levels of a non-cancerous liver tumor called hepatocleeular adenoma after being fed large amounts of Ritalin.

It is more than shocking also, that during the 1980's, the dramatic rise in Ritalin prescriptions coincided directly with Stephen Breuning's, M.D., fraudulent but significantly influential work "proving" that stimulant drugs such as Ritalin were solutions for hyperactivity. Although much of his work was fabricated and Dr. Breuning received a prison sentence for this fraud, thousands of parents and medical doctors are still influenced by his work and the number of stimulant prescriptions for children continues to rise.

In December, 1994, an article by Antonia Black, appeared in the Redbook magazine called "The Drugging of America's

Children." It stated that although the Physician's Desk Reference warns doctors not to prescribe Ritalin for children under six years old, over 200,000 prescriptions for Ritalin and other stimulant drugs were prescribed for children age 5 and under in 1993.

In response, Dr. Fred Baughman, a pediatric neurologist, asked a revealing and important question in the May 12, 1993, Correspondence section of the *American Medical Association Journal*. "What is the danger of having these children believe they have something wrong with their brains that makes it impossible for them to control themselves without a pill? What is the danger of having the most important adults in their lives, their parents and teachers, believe this as well?"

After careful examination of the entire issue we felt it important that we all ask exactly what price is too much to pay so that our children can concentrate and focus? Is it possible that other factors are creating the rise in the number of children given this ADHD label? Could it be that certain factors in our children's lifestyles actually contribute to the symptoms of a "learning disability?" Are there safer and more humane alternatives to drugging millions of children just so they can attend school? Are there other ways to achieve what we think is best for children which are more natural and time-honored?

As the parent of a son diagnosed with ADHD I have experienced first hand, the complete confusion and emotional exhaustion of finding the best answers to help my son. I knew from the beginning of his childhood that my son had special needs that might not be met in the traditional school setting. It was only after years of research, attending endless parent teacher meetings to request special accommodations for my son and even briefly filling his prescription for a stimulant drug that I knew there had to be a better way for all of us.

Throughout the years I have individually tutored hundreds of students whose parents shed tears of despair and helplessness because their children also could not fit into classrooms set up for "normal" children. When they received reports that their children could not learn through the traditional methods in the classroom (i.e., talk in turn, sit in seat, work on tasks within time limits) most of these parents began to believe that their children were definitely not "normal."

What they did not know initially, however, was that their children actually had very special creative abilities, but simply could not make the behavioral concessions necessary to reveal these abilities in the regular classroom. The result was that often, their children were placed in resource special education (RSP) programs because of poor academic performance. These parents were literally worn down from lack of success and not knowing where to turn. Drugs seemed like the only choice.

Dr. Hills and I wrote this book for parents, grandparents and teachers. We want to provide the kind of answers that do not require drugs and offer instead, solutions that may even allow your children to shed their learning disability label. We have spent many years learning how to help children develop their natural, innate learning abilities (without the use of drugs) and we want to pass these methods onto you.

What you will read is about compromises, changes and faith. You will learn about the compromises and changes you can make in your child's diet. Our hope is that you develop faith along the way. The faith to believe that your child is *capable*. Capable of learning, capable of making good decisions and capable of growing into an adult with radiant health, solid dignity and a sense of purpose.

Health and your child's wellness mean much more than having a child who can remain quiet long enough so the adults in his or her life can get something done. Health and wellness allow your child to be curious, vibrant, fully engaged in the task of new learning and able to live peacefully with the others in your family and school.

This book will open your eyes to the new information and possibilities that exist in the field of health and nutrition as they relate to your child's abilities to learn. There are documented medical studies that show dramatic changes in children's behavior and learning capabilities from such things as small adjustments in diet or the addition of certain supplements. One recent study has found vitamin B6 to be more effective than Ritalin at calming hyperactive children.

As you look for them, and develop a new mind-set, you will discover the things in your child's daily life that have the ability to masquerade as learning disability symptoms. You will learn how the lack of even minute amounts of minerals, vitamins and amino acids can create brain and body imbalances in your child. When brain functions are impaired, symptoms like memory loss, lack of concentration, and hyperactivity can result. Food sensitivities, allergies and intolerances will be the first place to begin your search. You will begin to notice that even your child's handwriting will change when specific foods to which your child is sensitive, are removed from his or her diet. Finding the hidden triggers that add to or create the appearance of learning problems in your child will open up a whole new realm of possibilities and can even result in your child's "disability" label being removed.

The medical community is now recognizing the direct links between diet and health. It takes many years of high fat, high sugar, low fiber diets to create a diseased body and incredible work to undo the damage. The changes being prescribed include diet, nutritional supplements, exercise and more responsible eating patterns. The good news is that you have a child who is still growing, and it is possible to implement those changes now.

Healthy eating and the proper use of supplements can significantly affect children's ability to learn now. All our major medical schools have established new research and treatment programs to allow patients to take control of their lives and learn preventive techniques that create health, rather than simply rely on drugs that focus on lessening the symptoms of poor health habits.

Most importantly, with this new knowledge, you and your child will discover a new sense of purpose in your lives. You can both take charge and create new solutions for yourselves and your family. These new paths will create health and wellness, and renewed faith in your child's natural abilities to learn.

Our book begins with the true story of a young man by the name of Brandon. Follow him throughout the book and discover the kinds of brain and body imbalances which caused him to be placed in a special education program for what appeared to be his inability to learn in math, reading and language. You will rejoice as you see him progress from "learning disabled" to normal functioning in the regular classroom following adjustments in his diet, needed supplementation and the love and caring of his family. We invite you to read on to Chapter 1...

--- Pat Wyman

Chapter 1

What's Food Got to Do With It?

Inadequate nutrition and learning disabilities are linked...

"To have a renewed body, you must be willing to have new perceptions that give rise to new solutions."

Deepak Chopra, M.D.

Brandon is an extremely active 12 year old. He eats doughnuts and frosted cereal for breakfast every day, and goes to school feeling great. After a while though, he gets tired and irritable and doesn't want to be there.

Brandon usually has the school lunch of pizza, coke and cookies, and hangs out with his friends at the local fast food place after school. All his teachers say he is very bright, but just can't concentrate on his work. Some days he seems attentive, but most days he doesn't finish his work, talks too much with his friends, and generally does poor quality work. When he comes home, it is a major problem to get him to do homework and he tells his parents that he just does not like to read. Besides, when he does read, he makes so many mistakes he can't even remember the information from page to page. He wonders why he should even go to school...

Case histories like Brandon's and the latest medical research in the area of nutrition make it very clear that nutrition can be both the cause of the symptoms *and* the remedy for many learning disabilities.   In fact, when certain changes in a child's diet are made and the proper supplements added, medical research has shown that I.Q. and other test scores have risen, memory abilities are enhanced and the overall ability to learn and remember improve dramatically.

Brandon is not truly learning disabled, but his symptoms made him appear that way in school and at home.   In fact, he was placed into some special resource classes because many academic tests showed scores more than two years below his grade level.   What neither his parents nor teachers knew at that time, however, was that Brandon actually had several food sensitivities and food allergies.   In addition, he was lacking certain minerals and amino acids which contributed to his problems in school.   The combination of these problems affected Brandon's ability to pay attention and often caused him to be over-active, sometimes "spacey", forgetful and irritable.

Once Brandon's hidden food allergies and nutrient deficiencies were discovered and treated, Brandon was able to return to his regular classes and experience academic success.   He regained his self-esteem and went on to high school to do very well.   As you read on, you will discover the true causes of Brandon's academic and behavioral problems and what the remedies are that improved his ability to learn.

The information in this book will help you determine exactly what part of your child's eating habits may be reducing his or her ability to learn. Once you have identified what your child needs, you will discover many natural sources to help your child maximize his or her brain power and make the job of learning and recalling new information a joyous event again.

Learning requires optimum health and brain function; if a child is eating the wrong foods or those foods which are deficient in the proper nutrients, his or her ability to learn will be compromised. The food and food supplements (vitamins, minerals and amino acids) you give to your child play a major role in whether he or she is successful in school and in life.

Making the connection between learning and nutrition is absolutely essential to understanding why millions of children each year (just like Brandon) are being burdened with the "learning disabled" label, when in fact, they are vitamin, mineral and amino acid deficient, hypersensitive to what they eat or drink or filled with metal toxins.

Take the inventory (Is This My Child?) on the next page to determine if your child's learning disabilities may be related to or caused by allergens, toxic metals or nutritional factors.

Is This My Child?

Answer The Following Questions To Determine If Your Child's Learning Disabilities May Be Due to Food Allergies, Metal Toxins, Vitamin, Mineral or Amino Acid Deficiencies, Pollutants, etc.

1. Was your child colicky and irritable during infancy?
2. Does your child experience temper tantrums, head banging or bed rocking?
3. Does your child wet the bed, beyond the age of twelve?
4. Did your child have repeated ear infections?
5. Has your child had several "rounds" of antibiotics or tubes put in his ears?
6. Is your child irritable, hyperactive, overactive or fidgety?
7. Does your child have frequent mood swings, or cry easily?
8. Has your child been given Ritalin, Dexedrine or other drugs to calm him or her down or to increase learning?
9. Is your child often depressed or tired?
10. Does he or she complain of headaches, stomach or muscle pain?
11. Does tobacco smoke, perfume or other chemical odors bother your child?
12. Is your child overweight/underweight and crave sweets, soft drinks or other junk foods?
13. Is your child bothered by nasal congestion or constant runny nose?
14. Does your child have black circles under his or her eyes, or pink and puffy eyes?
15. Does your child experience diarrhea or constipation?
16. Does your child seem dull, lethargic, and "spacey" and unable to follow directions?

If you answered yes to one or more questions, your child has some special needs and will benefit from modifying his/her nutritional program. Read on to find out why food may not be the only answer to increasing your child's learning power...

Why Our Food Cannot Give Us What We Need...

Most doctors will tell you that your child gets all the nutrition he or she needs from the food they eat. What you won't hear however, is how certain food along with all its additives, preservatives and fat content may also have serious negative effects on your child. Also, most medical doctors know very little about nutrition because it is not included in their curriculum. William Crook, M.D., a well known authority on hyperactivity and learning disabilities says, "What most doctors say about food and nutrition would be true for our ancestors who ate a variety of unrefined foods grown in soils which had not been treated with chemicals. But today, our children are urged by television to consume foods and beverages loaded with sugar and other "naked calories" (no vitamins and minerals)." [1]

Many medical doctors are generally unaware that our soil is so depleted that fresh fruits and vegetables do not have the mineral content that a healthy body needs. Basically, through poor crop rotation, loss of valuable topsoil due to flooding, and over irrigation, much of the natural trace mineral content has been lost from our food supply.

The United States Senate (in Senate Document 264, published in 1936) stated, "Our physical well-being is more directly dependent upon the minerals we take into our systems than upon calories or vitamins..."

It also stated that food produced on mineral deficient land was starving us of perfect health. "The alarming fact is that foods (fruits, vegetables and grains) now being raised on millions of acres of land that no longer contain enough of certain minerals are starving us - no matter how much of them we eat. No man of today (1936) can eat enough fruits and vegetables to supply his system with the minerals he requires for perfect health because his stomach isn't big enough to hold them."

Compared with the food in years past, our packaged food today is full of unnecessary, unwanted, and unpronounceable ingredients. The reasons are many - from marketing ploys to gain more of your dollars, to cost cutting in the manufacturing process. What it all adds up to however, is that the food your child eats is directly connected to his or her health, and ability to perform well in school. And since that food (even fresh) is also mineral deficient, your child cannot obtain enough of what he or she needs to stay healthy and alert for learning no matter how well he or she is eating. Your child will need more help and only you can give that help and information.

There is also much new medical information that chronic and degenerative diseases often take 30 or more years to develop. The medical community is prescribing more lifestyle changes and healthy eating patterns than ever before. Medical science now recognizes the connection between such things as stress, high fat, low fiber diets and the development of many diseases like heart disease and certain forms of cancer. Your doctor will tell you that these illnesses are seen after many years of eating high fat, and empty calorie diets. Arteries become clogged, digestion gets sluggish and the immune system is compromised.

You have the ability now to spare your child all of these types of illnesses by providing wellness and preventative care options from birth on. Educating your child about health will create a lifelong pattern for vital health throughout his or her life.

From Food To Mood

*"The real voyage of discovery consists
not in seeking new landscapes,
but in having new eyes. "*

Marcel Proust

Have you ever noticed that your child's moods and behavior are different after eating certain foods? Or maybe you notice that after eating a holiday meal with turkey and lots of pastas that your whole family feels relaxed and even tired. You will want to observe your child's responses to every kind of food and ask yourself whether your child's behaviors are a direct result of what he or she has eaten. Symptoms may show up immediately or up to one or two days later.

Food and your child's moods are very closely connected. Depending on the nutrient profile of each type of food, eating various foods can elevate your child's mood, make him or her tired, create hyperactivity or increase or decrease learning abilities. There are also many foods, even those that your child may like the most, that may be causing undetected allergic responses which can make the act of learning very difficult.

Marshall Mandell, M.D., a Clinical Ecologist, found that food allergies and poor mental performance were connected, and many learning disabilities may be actually due to food allergy in disguise.[1]

Over 200 of his patients were relieved of long-standing emotional complaints once specific allergens were removed from their diets. Dr. Mandell found that an 8 year old boy who fell asleep at his desk in the afternoon, and had been classified as a non-performer and hopeless daydreamer, was actually allergic to chocolate milk, ice cream, cupcakes, twinkies and chocolate chip cookies.

The child's breakfast consisted of two bowls of oat cereal every day and after testing, he was also found to be highly allergic to wheat gluten. Once all these foods were removed from his diet, the boy became a high achiever in school.

Although it is unclear exactly why, a high protein diet may have a calming effect on hyperactive children. Melvyn Werbach, M.D., author of *Healing Through Nutrition*, reports on two studies in the American Journal of Clinical Nutrition and the Journal of Nutrition, that "hyperactive children may need to eat more protein than other children because their bodies flush out nitrogen (which comes from protein) more readily."[2]

He also goes on to that "excessive amounts of protein could 'theoretically' promote cancer, kidney and heart disease' but it is not known whether a high-protein diet has 'long-term' adverse affects on health for hyperactive people who respond to the diet."

The wrong kinds of foods, those your child is allergic to, can rob your child of proper mental, emotional, physical and nutritional stability.   Many learning problems may be directly traced to certain trigger foods which can "alter pyschosocial behavior and perception", says Abram Hoffer, Ph.D., M.D.[3]

Do you remember your last holiday meal? If it included turkey, an amino acid called tryptophan was responsible for that relaxed, even tired feeling you had after eating. Carbohydrates (pastas, breads, cereals, etc.) also produce a tired, "want to sleep" feeling and may not be the best choice to feed your child right before going to school. Proteins, on the other hand, (eggs, cheese, fish, etc.) will increase alertness and memory and raise your child's mental abilities.

When you take the time to notice exactly what your child is eating, even during the school day, you may be surprised to find foods in the school cafeteria that can contribute to many learning disability symptoms. The following studies show the important connection between food and learning.

Changes in School Cafeteria Food
Result in 41% increase in national test scores!

One of the largest studies ever which showed how significantly diet affects learning was conducted in 803 of the New York City Public Schools in 1979-1983. One million school children were involved in the study which was based on the "Feingold" diet. Over a four year period, the schools eliminated artificial colors, flavors, preservatives like BHA and BHT, and reduced the amount of sugar in the cafeterias' food. To assess their learning progress, the children took the California Achievement Test the three years before and the four years during the study.

The results were spectacular! *The International Journal of Biosocial Research* published the study and the authors wrote, "In short, New York City Public Schools raised their mean national academic performance percentile rating from 39.2 percent to 54.9 percent in four years, with the gains occurring in the first, second and fourth years (precisely when the dietary improvements were made)."

What is also interesting is the fact that before the dietary changes, 12.4 percent of the one million student sample were performing two or more years below grade level. At the end of the study, that rate had dropped to 4.9 percent.

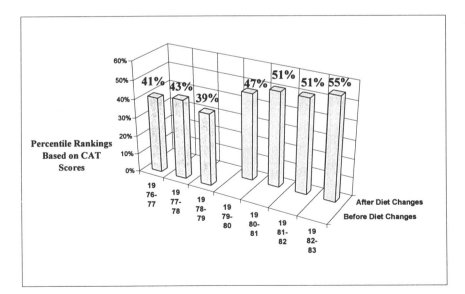

Increase in School Test Scores with Dietary Changes

Even more exciting is the fact that before the dietary changes, the fewer numbers of children who ate the school food, the higher the school's performance on the test. After the diet was changed, the higher number of children who ate school meals within each school, the greater that school's rate of gain in its ranking on the test.[4]

In addition, during the third year of the study, the children ate the same food as they had before the study and the gains from the previous year held constant. During the fourth year, the Feingold diet was implemented again and the national percentile ranking rose an additional 4 percent!

For more information on the Feingold Diet contact the Feingold Association at 1 (800) 321-3287.

The Foods That Spark
Learning Disability Symptoms

When your child experiences difficulty in school and with learning, they may develop emotional, physical or psychological symptoms. Each of these symptoms can be directly related to the central nervous system and can be thought of as "brain allergies." The brain can actually swell after certain allergic foods are eaten causing headaches, dizziness, weakness, anxiety, depression and visual and auditory hallucinations. In many cases the child's abilities to read and write can be severely affected. [5]

"Brain Allergy"

Read the following list to find the foods *most likely* to create abnormal learning patterns and symptoms in both children and adults. Use this list as a starting point when looking for possible food allergies in your child.

MILK. Contrary to the advertisements you may see, milk does not build strong bodies for everyone. Cow's milk leads the list of allergic symptoms in young children as well as school age children and adults. Many times a colicky baby will develop into a milk allergic child with upper respiratory problems and tubes in their ears at an early age. Stuffiness and irritability are major problems at an early age due to the allergic response to milk.

Milk may cause sinusitis, runny nose, mucus, constipation and/or diarrhea, and frequent colds because it cannot be digested. Animals, once weaned, do not ever drink milk again. If your child has puffy red eyes with black circles under them, pale color, nasal congestion, and other respiratory symptoms such as asthma; milk and cheese are usually the culprit. Try removing all milk products (cheese, pizzas, milk soups, margarine/butter, gravies, ice cream, puddings, and other foods with milk) from your child's diet for one month to see a dramatic difference.

CHOCOLATE. Chocolate is composed of toxic chemicals called "brown stuff" and may cause migraine headaches in both children and adults due to the theobromide. Chocolate is also known to alter moods due to the tryptophan which develops seratonin (a neurotransmitter) causing relaxation. If your child eats chocolate and has a sensitivity, he or she may become drowsy and unable to concentrate.

SUGAR. Sugar is a well known culprit in many learning disability cases because it robs the brain and body of all water-soluble vitamins and minerals. One vitamin which is lost, vitamin B, gives the cells energy needed for thinking, coordination and memory. When your child has sugar donuts or a sugar coated cereal before school, his blood sugar level will drop about 20 minutes after eating. This may cause forgetfulness, lack of oxygen to the brain, and affect the ability to concentrate. Sugar also allows the growth of bacteria which will ferment in the intestines and cause lack of digestion.

Refined sugar is particularly insidious since it produces a type of addiction as severe as any drug addiction. "Many adolescents will grab for sweets even though they notice that their behavior is normal when they avoid sugar and may be pathological when they consume it," according to Abram Hoffer, Ph.D., M.D., author of *Orthomolecular Nutrition*.[6] Sugar addiction provides typical addiction withdrawal symptoms as severe as those accompanying withdrawal from drugs.

"Sugar that has been appropriated from the sugar cane and the beet, leaves behind vitamins and minerals and are nutritionally empty caloric intruders." Sugar robs vitamins and mineral nutrition from the cells. "The effect is similar to that of an unannounced guest showing up for dinner. The good hostess, in order to satisfy the guest, borrows from the others in the family, in the case of cells, vitamins and minerals," says Dr. Leonard Hippchen.[7]

Dr. Hippchen goes on to say that "Behavior can be affected by what we eat as well as by what we fail to obtain and...continuation of a nutritionless diet, (robbed by sugar) undermines physical and mental vitality, a major cause of underachieving and fatigue."

In his book, *Healing Through Nutrition*, Melvyn Werbach, M.D. says that sugar can interfere with learning by increasing adrenaline levels. He notes that, "In a Yale study, children, but not adults, had a dramatic rise in blood adrenaline after eating the equivalent of two frosted cupcakes for breakfast. Adrenaline may increase anxiety and irritability and reduce concentration, thus making learning more difficult."[8]

WHEAT. With the advent of hybridizing wheat for greater yield, the pesticides and toxins that are sprayed on it stay in the wheat germ. Wheat today is unlike the wheat of 50 years ago in that these pesticides become part of its molecular structure and may cause a chemical, allergic reaction in susceptible children.   The protein in wheat, called gluten, causes digestive problems because it coats the villi in the intestines and prevents digestion.   Gluten feeds yeast in the intestines which in turn causes bacterial invasions and digestive malabsorption, i.e. stomach aches.

Symptoms of behavior changes from wheat allergies may include decreased pupil size, decreased motor skills, epileptic seizures, interrupted sleep, apathy, decreased coordination, sore muscles, diarrhea, gas, and impairment in the functions of the small intestines in digestion.   Undigested food escapes into the bloodstream alerting the immune system and histamines to fight off the offending particles; thus an allergy develops.

NITRATES.   "Nitrite is believed to be the most toxic chemical in the nation's food supply," according to Dr. Leonard J. Hippchen, former chairman of the American Correctional Association's Committee on Classification and Treatment.   It is added to seven billion pounds of food each year.   It preserves colors and increases flavor.   It keeps the ham pink, but it can also block oxygen transport (known as methemoglobinemia)."

"Found in hot dogs, lox, bacon, ham, luncheon meats, smoked fish, salami, corn dogs and bologna, nitrates can cause stomach pain, blurry eyes, and brain fog. Children under the age of 1 year are so sensitive to it that it is no longer included in baby products. Nitrates and nitrites are considered to be the most potentially dangerous carcinogenic source." There are also studies which link nitrates to leukemia in children.

MSG. We can't say anything good about monosodium glutamate. It is a chemical that increases taste acuity. MSG can cause headaches, swelling and the inability to concentrate. It can make children dizzy, aggressive, angry, drowsy and can also cause them to have irregular heart beats. Many people have reported nausea, skin problems, hair loss, insomnia, mental and nervous system disorders. Psychological, neurological and emotional disorders have also been reported after eating foods with MSG in them.

Both authors have had acute reactions to MSG, including migraines and blurry vision. These kinds of reactions were originally called the Chinese Restaurant Syndrome. As far back as 1969, Dr. John Olney, of the Washington School of Medicine, reported that injections of MSG damaged the central nervous system of infant mice and rats. Learning disabilities, obesity, dwarfism, behavioral disturbances and retinal defects have been reported with its use.

CAFFEINE. Melvyn Werbach, M.D. reports in his book, *Healing Through Nutrition* that "since high levels of caffeine consumption may cause anxiety, depression, and various symptoms, too much caffeine is likely to interfere in learning. Evidence of this relationship comes from a survey of college students which found heavy caffeine consumers had poorer grades." Cola drinks, coffee and other sugar drinks with caffeine elevate the blood sugar and drop it suddenly a few minutes later causing the same problems as sugar. Children and adults can get irritable, aggressive, disruptive, and display a short attention span.

Nervousness and hyperactivity can often result from the use of caffeine and female adult women often report cystic breasts after using caffeine.

"My high school age daughter", says co-author Pat Wyman, "came home from school one afternoon and said that a friend had shared a cold tea drink with her (the kind that comes in bottles) at lunch that day. She told me how jittery she was during all of her afternoon classes that day and how much it affected her ability to concentrate."

**DANGER! FATS AND OILS**! Any foods with hydrogenated or partially hydrogenated oils allow free radicals (which may cause disease of all kinds) to roam throughout the body.   Free radicals are simply molecules that are missing an electron and desperately trying to snatch one from any other molecule.   As they do this they actually terrorize the molecules in the body.   Free radicals can be neutralized by antioxidants, compounds that give up one of their electrons, thus returning the free radicals to normal.

If you look at nearly every packaged food, you will see that it has hydrogenated or partially hydrogenated fat in it. Hydrogenated simply means that it has been converted from liquid to solid form.   Jean Carper, author of *Stop Aging Now*, says this of oils: "If you want to age fast, eat the type of fat (hydrogenated or partially hydrogenated) that turns into a free radical factory in your body, making your cells dysfunctional, cancerous, wantonly destructive and suicidal. Eating the wrong fats sets off fierce chain reactions in which free radicals rip through your cells, mutilating and draining them of life.   The fats you let into your body are key to how fast you age and the diseases that may overtake you."[9]

Fats become oxidized when they are exposed to oxygen. When it is set out, vegetable oil such as corn oil, becomes infused with oxygen within two or three seconds and ravaged with free radicals, says free radical researcher, Harry Demopoulos, M.D., formerly a professor at New York University and now president of Antioxidant Pharmaceuticals Corporation in New York.   Once you or your child ingest the oil, the most dangerous "lipid hydroperoxide" free radical molecules are like a time bomb in your body setting off a chain reaction destroying your body's cells.

SERVE ONLY MONOUNSATURATED OILS to protect your child's body. Olive oil, flaxseed oil and macadamia nut oil are the best because they have omega-3 fatty acids which are necessary for breaking down protein.

THE MARGARINE MYTH

According to Jean Carper, author of *Stop Aging Now*, eating margarine is one of the reasons why the United States is 17th in life expectancy. Margarine is the prime carrier of trans fatty acids that make cells function abnormally. Some safflower oils have been modified to make them monounsaturated and therefore safe for you to consume. Check the labels of each food you give to your child and yourself.

Most prepackaged food has fat that tends to turn rancid - crackers, baked goods, cereals, sauces, salad oils, mayonnaise, pizza and puddings. Even frozen foods can contain these polyunsaturated and hydrogenated (converted from liquid to solid) oils that will rob you of your health.

Free radicals can also originate from outside the body from smoking, pollution, too much sunlight and exposure to environmental chemicals. Limit your family's exposure to all of these.

Other foods that trigger learning disability symptoms are: wheat, corn, soy, eggs and citrus. These can cause behavioral problems, diarrhea and intermittent constipation.

Important Relationship Found Between Diet and ADD/ADHD Symptoms.

There is much new scientific evidence to support the relationship between diet and ADD/ADHD (Attention Deficit Disorder and Attention Deficit Hyperactivity Disorder) symptoms. William Crook M.D., in his booklet *"Hyperactivity and The Attention Deficit Disorder"*, describes a double-blind placebo-control study by Boris and Mandel, published in the May 1994 Annals of Allergy.

Twenty-six children diagnosed with ADD/ADHD were tested in their own homes on a break from school, and placed on an elimination diet. The foods that were eliminated were those most known to cause allergic symptoms - dairy, wheat, corn, yeast, soy, citrus, egg, chocolate and peanuts, as well as artificial colors and preservatives.

The children showed significant improvement on the elimination diet and their symptoms returned when the offending foods were added back to their diets.

Also, a Purdue University study by Stevens, Zentall, Abate, Kuczek and Burgess as reported in the June, 1996 issue of Physiology and Behavior, found that "A greater number of behavior problems were reported in subjects with lower total omega-3 fatty acid concentrations. Additionally, more learning and health problems were found in subjects (boys, ages 6-12) with lower total omega-3 fatty acid concentrations."

An article by A.P. Simopoulos in the September 1991 Journal of Clinical Nutrition points out why the American diet is deficient in omega-3 fatty acids. Humans evolved with a 1:1 ratio of omega-6 and omega-3 fatty acids. About 100 years ago, the vegetable industry began to hydrogenate oil, which caused the oil's omega-3 content to be reduced. In addition, the livestock industry began to use feed grains which were lower in omega-3's but high in omega-6 fatty acids. The final result is that the American diet now has an essential fatty acid ratio of 20-25:1 omega-6 to omega-3 rather than the 1:1 healthy ratio that we need to keep cholesterol low.

For symptoms of an omega-3 fatty acid deficiency look for tiny lumps on the back of your child's arm, increased allergies, increased thirst, frequent urination, dry skin and hair, brittle nails and acne. Giving your child evening primrose oil will help correct this.

Yeast: Too Much of A Good Thing

Years ago, William Crook, M.D., wrote a wonderful book called *The Yeast Connection*. Although it is now out of print, it helped millions of people by describing the connection between a yeast overgrowth, learning problems, hyperactivity and a variety of certain types of illnesses. Due to repeated doses of antibiotics, children may develop an overgrowth of yeast which then masquerades as the symptoms of a learning disability. The real cause of their symptoms may not be correctly traced to the overgrowth of yeast.

Yeasts are microscopic spores and Dr. Crook says, "one family of yeasts, Candida albicans, lives normally on the dark interior membranes of a person's body - especially in the digestive tract and vagina. Candida occurs both as a single-cell yeast and as a branching fungus."[10]

When a child takes repeated doses of antibiotic drugs (or even one course) the friendly bacteria in his or her digestive tract gets eliminated. Yeasts multiply because they are not affected by antibiotics. When these friendly bacteria are wiped out, candida takes over and can cause diarrhea, constipation, thrush in the mouth and genitals, diaper rash or vaginitis. More importantly, yeast products are released into the bloodstream and cause countless physical, mental and nervous system disorders, including hypoglycemia.

Some of the symptoms your child may experience from Candida albicans are: muscle aches, cramps, gas, bloating, digestive upsets, diarrhea, headaches, blurred vision, hyperactivity, anxiety, fatigue, low blood pressure, low blood sugar, sore throats, and inability to concentrate.

Dr. Crook and many other physicians have had great success treating Candida albicans with a special elimination diet and antifungal prescription medications such as nystatin. Health food stores also carry several products which help to restore the yeast balance such as *Yeast Fighters* by Twinlab and caprylic acid products (Mycopryl, Capricin and Caprystatin). In addition, Dr. Crook recommends Kyolic garlic.

Recently, Dr. Crook has written a new book, *The Yeast Connection Handbook,* which contains the latest information and research on the relationship between Candida albicans and a large variety of health problems. It is a highly regarded and helpful book you will want to read time and again as you search for answers to you and your children's health needs. You may also want to share Dr. Crook's book with your family physician who may be open to learning more about yeast. Appendix A in his book includes a special message from Dr. Crook to physicians.

If you suspect that your child has a yeast connected health or learning problem, you will want to reduce or eliminate the sugar that your child eats. Sugar feeds the yeast and causes an overgrowth.

Of course, the first thing you will want to know is what you can use in place of the sugar. There are several items on the market that can be easily obtained. These are: FOS -

fructooligosaccharides, stevia, pure liquid saccharin, rice syrup and fructose powder.

FOS allows the growth of beneficial bacteria and interferes with the growth of harmful types. Unfortunately, FOS is still quite expensive, but you can find it in powder form or capsule.

Although we mention stevia a bit later in the book, we'll also include it here. It is an herbal product from the perennial shrub of the aster family that has been used for centuries in South America and used by millions of people in China and Japan. We buy it at the health food store (it is still classified as a supplement) and both our families use it. It comes in a powdered form and you need just a tiny bit because it is many times sweeter than sugar.

Although much controversy still surrounds the use of saccharin, newer medical research shows no connection to illness or cancer causing responses in lab animals. Liquid saccharin can be found in almost every grocery or drug store. Rice syrup and fructose powder are relatively inexpensive and can be easily found in the health food store.

Good News for Parents with ADD/ADHD and Autistic Children.

Dr. William Crook reports exciting new findings in his booklet, *Hyperactivity and the Attention Deficit Disorder*. He says that in 1995, studies by William Shaw, Ph.D., report the finding of fungal metabolites in the urine of 18 autistic children. Over 75% of the children gave a history of frequent infections which had been treated with antibiotics. Once treatment was started with oral antifungal medications (Nystatin, Nizoral or Diflucan) for seven days, the lab findings returned to normal and the children showed significant improvement!

In August, 1995, Dr. Shaw found similar fungal metabolites in the urine of children with ADD/ADHD. This strongly suggests that antifungal medication and a sugar free diet can help thousands of children with ADD/ADHD who have a history of multiple antibiotic use.

One final word on foods and your child's mood. It is only your detective work that will begin to educate your child on the connection between food, behavior, learning and lifelong health. Remember that you are giving your child a gift for life as you teach sound eating habits and preventive wellness. Diseases do not develop overnight; often they take 20 or 30 years to show up in the body. Your work now may save your child heart problems and other types of degenerative diseases later in life.

Chapter 3

The Coca Pulse Test for Food Allergies

*"If we all did the things we are capable of doing,
we would literally astound ourselves."*

Thomas A. Edison

If you suspect that food allergies may be the cause of your child's disabilities, inappropriate behavior or poor performance in school, Arthur F. Coca, M.D. has developed a simple pulse test to determine whether food allergies are present. [1]

Before you begin, you will want to know that locating the pulse of a younger child is often quite difficult. Their pulse tends to be irregular and faster than you might think normal. We recommend that you take your child's pulse before he or she gets out of bed for three days in a row and then divide by 3 to get an approximate baseline number. When your child awakens in the morning, take his or her pulse before moving or getting out of bed. Using your second and third fingers (not your thumb) at the base of the wrist, measure the number of beats you feel in 60 seconds. Dr. Coca recommends that you use a stop watch and measure the beats for a full 60 seconds.

After your child gets dressed, take his or her pulse again. (This is done before eating while in a sitting position.)

Add both pulses and divide by 2. The answer equals your child's normal daily pulse rate.

Using the Food Log found at the end of this chapter, have your child eat one food only, and then take your child's pulse after 30 minutes, 60 minutes and 90 minutes while in a sitting position. (This is probably best done on the weekend when your child can rest quietly or watch a calming movie or t.v. program between the tests. It is also important to not let your child listen to any type of fast music which will speed up the heart rate). Record the information on the log.

If your child's pulse rises or falls 10 points above or below the base level, he or she is allergic to that food.

You must keep the log and take your child's pulse for at least 6 days in a row while making sure that your child does not eat the same foods every day. This way, you will get a very accurate reading of your child's minimum and maximum pulse each day. From there, when the pulse rises or falls due to a food allergy, you will know the normal range for the pulse and the allergy will be easier to detect.

Each day, try this technique with one new food, and make sure to remember to rotate the foods every four days, not eating the same foods twice in a row.   Theron G. Randolph, M.D., author of *Human Ecology and Susceptibility to the Chemical Environment* says, " It takes four days for any food or chemical to be entirely eliminated from the human system."

By rotating the foods in your child's diet, he or she will not experience an allergy to a certain food every single day. Often, physical and mental reactions to the chemicals in your child's foods lessen in intensity when your child does not eat them for four days. When the substance is reintroduced, your child may experience even more acute symptoms. The other alternative is to eliminate that food entirely from your child's diet.

Reasonably speaking, however, in today's fast paced life, it is often simpler to rotate the foods for your child due to the fact that he or she may become "addicted" and crave the very foods that they are allergic to. However, many children cannot ever tolerate certain foods and chemicals in foods, and should not be permitted to eat them, according to William H. Philpott, M.D., author of *Brain Allergies, The Psychonutrient Connection.*

If you wish to test for food coloring sensitivities, place 1 drop of certified coloring in a teaspoon of bottled water and give it to your child. Red, yellow and blue should be tested. Green does not need to be tested because it is a combination of yellow and blue.

CAUTION! It is a good idea to test these colorings about one week apart. Some children may experience a significant reaction like anger, anxiety, phobias, headaches, stomach cramps, blurry vision, or violent behavior. If there is a reaction, have the child take one teaspoon of baking soda in a half glass of water or juice as the antidote.

Sample Food Log

Food Eaten	Pulse Rate:	30 Minutes	60 Minutes	90 Minutes
Tomatoes				
Eggs				
Bread				
Cheese				
Corn				
Chocolate				
Milk				

Chapter 4

The Hidden Triggers

Food Allergies and Sensitivities

*"What good is inspiration if it's
not backed up by action?"*

Anthony Robbins

Each year, thousands more children, just like Brandon in Chapter 1, are being labeled as "learning disabled." During the 1970's Dr. Ben Feingold, an allergist who wrote *Why Your Child is Hyperactive*, said that our country was seeing 10 to 20 times as many kids with hyperactivity and learning difficulty as we were seeing 20 years ago.

Today, 25 years later, those numbers are much higher. In addition, several more categories have been added to the special education descriptions. The learning disability term has come to mean everything from hyperactive or brain damaged to emotionally disturbed. For parents and teachers, it means that the child is functioning two or more years below grade level in either specific subject areas or behavioral indicators.

The increase in the numbers of children with learning disabilities is startling. Every day, in some newspaper or magazine, we see reports about millions of children being put on medication, just to be able to cope with everyday life. According to Joel Wallach, N.D., 1991 Nobel Prize Nominee, "as many as 80% of 'dyslexic' kids are really suffering from food allergies and/or sugar sensitivity (where the sugar acts as a drug and produces a pharmacological effect just like speed)." He goes on to say, "these food sensitivities create learning disabilities that 'mimic' organic disease and too many salvageable kids are put on drugs (i.e. Ritalin), shunted off into "special education programs or worse yet, given up on as lost by frightened, frustrated families. Food allergies and sensitivities should be seriously investigated and dealt with, if these children are to have a fair shot at a normal life." [1]

In Dr. William G. Crook's booklet called *Hyperactivity and the Attention Deficit Disorder*, he says, "When I began practicing pediatrics in 1949, I knew absolutely nothing about hidden food allergies. Yet today, I know beyond any shadow of a doubt that most children who are troubled by hyperactivity and other symptoms which make them hard to raise, react to foods they are eating every day."

Another physician, Doris Rapp, M.D., a pediatric allergist and author of *Is This Your Child?* and *Is This Your Child's World?*, discovered over 20 years ago that food allergies and sensitivities can cause a very long list of symptoms which are just like those of Attention Deficit Hyperactivity Disorder. She has had dramatic success treating ADD/ADHD children by uncovering food and environmental allergies/sensitivities and will conduct phone consultations. She also provides a list of doctors experienced in treating children with ADHD/ADD. Call (716) 875-0398.

We have often seen children who exhibit many learning disability type symptoms and even uncontrollable behavior when given certain foods to which they are allergic or sensitive. These sensitivities are so evident that the child's handwriting changes drastically whenever they eat the culprit food. Dr. Mary Ann Block, author of *No More Ritalin,* displays the handwriting of some of her patients in her book. It is astounding to see the changes in handwriting of children undergoing food allergy/sensitivity testing. Many teachers will verify daily differences in their student's writing, although they may not know that it is food related.

Writing can be reversed, upside down, up or down-hill, completely illegible and then normal, all with different dilutions of suspected allergens.

Food allergy and food sensitivity testing are somewhat different, although the child's behavior and symptoms are similar. An allergy results in specific immediate reactions like swelling, hives, restricted breathing, etc. A sensitivity is delayed-onset and symptoms may show up either immediately or up to several days later.

When a doctor tests for an allergy he or she is typically looking for an antibody known as IgE which stands for immunoglobulin E and refers to the class to which the immunoglobulin belongs. A food sensitivity however, is categorized under IgG (immunoglobulin G) antibody reaction to food. Several studies in the medical literature (Lancet, Pediatrics and Annals of Allergy) reveal a specific association between behavior and the foods eaten, yet many allergists and physicians have not yet researched their significance.

Many physicians will not consider food allergies to be very significant simply because a person may not have an immediate reaction. However, in watching children everyday, their responses to certain foods are no less real or significant and can often wreak havoc in their school and home life. These sensitivities deserve attention and will often reveal the underlying causes of a child's disability symptoms. Once discovered and attended to, we have seen hundreds of children become suddenly "normal" in the eyes of their teachers and parents.

What is different? What is happening to cause this dramatic rise in numbers of children who simply cannot assimilate learning like the children in the past? Ask any teacher, and you will hear concerns about the children's' abilities to learn for as much as a quarter or more of the class.

The differences may actually begin as early as infancy when children are fed commercial baby food containing chemically modified starch and sugar. In a recent article in the San Francisco Chronicle (June 26, 1996), it is interesting to note that a major baby food manufacturer is finally going to eliminate the additives from its baby food. In the past, Gerber has put sugar and chemically modified starch into it's products, but has recently come under attack by consumer advocacy groups that complained about widespread deception regarding the nutritional content of Gerber's products.

Other reasons for the dramatic rise in "learning disabled" children may be the significant changes in how our food is grown and the types of pesticides sprayed on them. More than fifty years ago, our food was being grown in rich, fertile soil and free of the pesticides which can cause countless illnesses.

Yet another problem may arise due to chemical pollutants. "My own son, who is now fourteen, says co-author, Pat Wyman, was found to have large amounts of malathion in his body, due to the rampant spraying done in Southern California over 10 years ago. He was also diagnosed as ADHD (Attention Deficit Disorder without Hyperactivity) and was prescribed stimulant medication. Although it was against our better judgment, we put him on the medication for a brief time because he was having such difficulties concentrating and could barely remember any of his school assignments."

"Although some of his ability to concentrate improved, the side effects were very difficult to handle. He lost ten pounds (and was already thin), could not sleep and went to bed after 1:00 a.m. each morning. He also developed a facial tic. You can imagine the pain of watching all these things happen. I felt an enormous sense of guilt because I was so committed to using natural, drug-free treatments whenever possible."

"We took J.P. off the medication, gave him a hair analysis and put him on amino acid therapy (which you will read about in chapter 7). He was already taking minerals and vitamins and his hair analysis revealed some significant copper and aluminum toxicity. (You will read about these in later chapters). We added specific remedies to remove the excess copper and aluminum from his system and did not allow him to drink any more from aluminum cans."

"His return to normalcy was remarkable. After a period of about three weeks of being tired while clearing his system of the medication, we enjoyed watching him regain his personality, which had been dulled by the medication. We met with each of his teachers and were told that he was doing very well in school, remembering to write down all his assignments and turning them in on time. His grades went up and each day we are in awe of how he unfolds and blooms anew."

"Whether a relationship exists between the pesticide malathion and the ADHD is not clear, but it is my opinion that the pesticide in his body is certainly not helpful to him." In their new book, *Our Stolen Future,* Colburn, Dumanoski and Myers reveal more than 51 known chemicals (out of the thousands in use everyday) that definitely disrupt our endocrine systems, which are responsible for metabolism, growth and reproduction.

Several other causes of the rise in learning disabilities may be attributed to: the limited attention spans connected to watching television, the urbanization of society and increased drug, tobacco and alcohol use by women who are pregnant.

Food Additives, Preservatives and Colorings

Dr. Ben Feingold's research has certainly contributed significantly to our understanding of how food additives and colorings adversely affect our children's abilities to learn. He presented his findings to the American Medical Association as far back as 1973.

Dr. Feingold's work is related to the fact that food colorings and food additives often cause physical symptoms in children who are allergic or susceptible to these substances. In one of Dr. Feingold's studies, he took 23 hyperactive San Francisco school children and placed them on a diet which eliminated all artificial flavors, colors and food additives.   Fifteen of those children improved   so dramatically that Dr. Feingold went on to conduct most of the world's research studies on food colorings and food additives for the next several years.   He attributed most of the hyperactive symptoms we now call ADHD specifically to an allergic brain reaction to chemicals called "salicylates". These chemicals are found in the flavoring and coloring agents (there are over 3,000 of them) commonly used in convenience foods that are the mainstay of most children's diets.

There are also many foods that contain natural salicylates and if your child reacts to colorings or additives, it would be best to avoid such foods as: almonds, apples (cider and cider vinegars), apricots, blackberries, cherries, cloves, cucumbers and pickles, currants, gooseberries, grapes or raisins, mint flavors, nectarines, oranges, peaches, plums or prunes and raspberries.

In the *Medical Tribune*, Dr. Feingold is quoted as saying, "Many a child whose behavior baffles pediatricians, psychologists, educators and other professionals, will improve dramatically when they are put on a diet which eliminates artificial flavors and colors and other food additives."

Dr. Feingold finally concluded, "… our kids are consuming 10 times as much pop and other artificially flavored drinks as they used to, thus the increase in learning disabilities and hyperactivity is coincident with the addition of chemicals and additives in foods, and the increase in consumption." [2]

Foods with colorings, additives and preservatives (salicylates - as an aspirin derivative) can cause hyperactivity, other allergic reactions, abdominal pain, muscle aching, recurrent colds and bedwetting. Colorings and additives are in breakfast cereal, soft drinks, fruit ades, hot dogs, luncheon meat and ice cream. Cereal with BHA and BHT (rancid taste retardants) are especially bad offenders. BHA and BHT are also in potato chips, corn chips, peanuts, popcorn and hundreds of other foods.

Mineral Deficiencies Connected to Learning Disabilities

Proper mineral absorption is one of the major keys to eliminating or minimizing many of the learning disabilities diagnosed today. Minerals (major and trace) are often overlooked, yet are absolutely essential for optimum health. Minerals are the fundamentals of the bones, teeth, muscles, soft tissue, blood and nerve cells. They are important factors in maintaining body and brain processes, strengthening skeletal structures, and preserving the vigor of the heart and brain as well as muscle and nerve systems. Vitamins cannot even do their work without minerals because minerals assist vitamins to grow and repair tissue, furnish the body with heat and energy and assist in all the regulation of body processes.

Calcium, magnesium, phosphorus, potassium, sodium, chlorine and sulfur are known as the primary or major minerals. Other minerals, named trace minerals, are present in the body only in the most minute quantities, but are indispensable for proper body functioning.

Minerals are vital to overall mental and physical well being. Children who are classified as "learning disabled" are most often found lacking in one or more minerals. Merrill S. Read, M.D. former Director of the Growth and Development Branch of the National Institute of Child Health and Development, has devoted his entire life to the study of how nutrition affects children. He found apathetic children who had eaten no breakfast, were unable to pay attention, and who were disruptive in the classroom.   He identified the "nervous" children and gave them the mineral calcium as a supplement. It calmed them down immediately. Positive responses developed with just minimal efforts at nutritional improvements.

In another group of studies, Hugh Powers, M.D., as quoted in "Academic Therapy" found failing children and blamed their diets. [3] He limited carbohydrates, sugar, coffee, tea, and cola drinks. He added digestive enzymes to enhance the use of protein in their diets and added concentrated Vitamin B and C supplements. All of the students went from failing to become "A" and "B" students.

The following conditions have been found to be associated with certain mineral deficiencies. Be aware that these conditions may also be due to other causes.

Calcium - irritability, nervousness, depression, hyperactivity, nerve and muscle control, stunted growth, arthritis, muscle cramps, palpitations, tooth decay, brittle fingernails, etc.

Carbon - waste materials not burned up properly, respiration problems and changes in acid/alkaline balance in the body.

Chlorine - dizziness and roaring in the head, muscle tension and twitches, aching bones, stitches in the side during physical activity, bloating, digestive problems, inflamed lungs and throat.

Cobalt - pernicious anemia, brain cell damage, impaired immunity, emaciation and tissue atrophy.

Chromium - anxiety, fatigue, hypoglycemia, diabetes, retarded growth, high cholesterol.

Copper - depression, diarrhea, fatigue, fragile bones, anemia, balding, skin sores, eczema.

Iodine - hypothyroidism (low thyroid), slow mental reactions, low body temperature (below 97.8, slow metabolism, goiter, obesity.

Iron - irritability, dull mental processes, headaches, pale skin, anemia, lack of appetite, abnormal fatigue, shortness of breath, confusion, depression, dizziness, headaches, and anorexia.

Lithium - manic depression, high blood pressure, diabetes.

Magnesium - excessive irritability of nerves and muscles, nervous tics and twitches, irregular heartbeat, anxiety/confusion, restlessness, depression, hyperactivity, insomnia, muscle pain and weakness, and SIDS (Sudden Infant Death Syndrome).

Manganese - memory loss, anorexia, impaired judgment, weakness of ligaments and tendons, ataxia (muscular incoordination), hypoglycemia, tinnitis.

Molybdenum - excessive dental cavities.

Phosphorus - anxiety, apprehension, anorexia, irritability, fatigue, numbness, mental and physical fatigue, weakness, weight loss, pyorrhea, irregular breathing.

Potassium - intellectual/emotional/perceptual impairment, depression, nervousness, glucose intolerance, constipation, insomnia, heart palpitations, fast heart beat, fatigue, acne.

Selenium - ADD, ADHD, cystic fibrosis, impaired immunity, cataracts, growth retardation, muscular dystrophy, "heart attack", dandruff. A 1996 study in JAMA showed strong evidence that selenium may offer protection against cancer as well.

Silicon - bone and teeth problems, skeletal problems, osteoporosis.

Sulfur - eczema, arthritis, psoriasis, dermatitis, unhealthy hair, fingernails and skin.

Sodium - confusion, crying tantrums, headaches, depression, fatigue, memory loss, seizures, weight loss, taste loss, lethargy, infections, lethargy, flatulence, nausea.

Vanadium - diabetes, hypoglycemia, ADD, ADHD, Tuberculosis, hardening of bones.

Zinc - hyperactivity, memory loss, white spots on the nails, loss of taste and smell, depression, apathy, slow wound healing, irritability, acne, anorexia, brittle nails, fatigue.

Metal Toxicity is closely tied to learning disabilities.

Aluminum

In his book, *Healing Through Nutrition*, Melvyn Werbach, M.D., discusses the information found in several studies which closely tie metal toxicity to learning disabilities. He says, "Findings of several studies suggest that aluminum toxicity may play a role in learning problems. For example, serum aluminum levels were higher in 28 children with learning disorders or hyperactivity than in a group of normal children. Similarly, hair aluminum has been found to be elevated in some of the studies of dyslexic or learning disabled children." [4]

Other symptoms of aluminum toxicity may be G.I. irritations, motor paralysis, colic, nausea and skin ailments.

Aluminum toxicity is the result of drinking from aluminum cans, drinking water with high aluminum content, eating food with pesticides and additives in the soil, daily use of deodorants with high aluminum content, eating baked goods with baking powder on a regular basis, and heavy pollution.

Check the health food stores for a good deodorant without aluminum.

Arsenic

In the Journal of Forensic Medicine, Dr. H. A. Shapiro states that excess arsenic may cause various central nervous system disorders, headaches, convulsions, dehydration, skin eruptions, and garlic breath (in cases of arsenic poisoning). [5]

Cadmium and Lead

In the *Journal of Learning Disabilities*, Thatcher and Lester found that when 26 dyslexic children, aged 6-14, were compared to normal children, "they tended to have higher lead and cadmium concentrations both in their sweat and hair. Similarly, when 150 unselected school children were evaluated, the higher either their hair lead or hair cadmium levels, the lower their scores on measures of intelligence." [6]

Of all the medical evidence against these toxic metals, the strongest is for lead. In the *Journal of the American Medical Association*, 24 scientific studies were statistically analyzed. The authors' conclusion presented strong evidence that even low-level lead exposure impairs children's intelligence. [7]

When the diet is low in calcium, iron, copper and zinc, there may be a higher accumulation of lead in the tissues. When you add these minerals to your child's diet, it decreases the absorption of lead. Also, both thiamin (Vitamin B-1) and Vitamin C combat the effects of lead poisoning.

Sources of cadmium toxicity are refined foods, coffee, tea, processed meats, soft water, cola drinks, candies, refined cereals and grains and metal water pipes.

Sources of lead toxicity are paints with lead, enamels, glass, ink printing materials, lead crystal, crayons, and many anti-dandruff shampoos . Drinking water can also be quite toxic with high levels of lead. High lead levels have been found in over 100,000 school drinking fountains. The water itself may not naturally contain lead, but it can be transferred from lead plumbing to the water. It is good to have the pipes checked at your child's school.

Also, be sure and check the year your house was built. If it was built before 1979, purchase a lead test kit to determine whether lead was used in your interior or exterior paint. If you find that lead is present, The Center for Disease Control recommends a blood test done for each member of your family. A reading of 1 to 10 micrograms of lead per deciliter of blood is acceptable.

A lengthy article in the San Francisco Chronicle (December 16, 1996, Business Extra) revealed the long term effects of lead poisoning. These included learning disabilities, decreased growth, brain damage and even death in children.

According to the California Department of Health services, the article quoted that "250,000 children in California have elevated blood levels of lead. Symptoms include stomachaches, loss of appetite, decreased interest in play and excessive activity, fussiness or irritability."

Good safety tips include cleaning pacifiers and bottles after they fall to the floor, washing hands before meals and at bedtime, and keeping children away from any painted surfaces.

If you have a computer and access to the Internet, there are several sites with information about lead. Check the Consumer Product Safety Commission at www.cpsc.gov and the U.S. Environmental Protection Agency at www.epa.gov/opptintr/lead.

Mercury

Mercury concentrates in the brain, liver, kidneys and lungs and toxicity usually comes from pollution, dental amalgams in sensitive individuals, ointments, water based paints, antiseptics, camera film, fabric softener, floor waxes, fluorescent lamps, plastics and diuretics.

Organic mercury excesses can cause headaches, fatigue, dizziness, diarrhea, clumsiness, ataxia, nervousness, impaired concentration and memory, hearing defects and concentric visual field defects.

Individual toxic metal tests can be ordered by your doctor or a more detailed report can be obtained by a hair analysis which also includes nutrient mineral levels.

Read on to Chapter 5 to find out how to correct any mineral deficiencies your child may have.

HOW TO ELIMINATE TOXIC METALS
FROM THE BODY

Elizabeth Rees, M.D., a world-renowned pediatrician, who specialized in learning disabilities, offers a formula for metal detoxification in the Journal of Orthomolecular Psychiatry. [8]

1/2 cup homemade applesauce
1/2 cup kidney, black beans, aduki beans, white beans, or navy beans
1 capsule of 500 mg. L-methionine
3 Multimins capsules (we use Twinlab brand)
5 Kelp Tablets

Take all the capsules in divided doses during the day. The beans may be served in salad or alone and the applesauce may be taken at any time during the day.

Children should be served each of the above daily for a week. Check to make sure that your child has no food allergy to beans or applesauce first.

A hair analysis must be completed first in order to determine the presence of any toxic metals in the body. It may be repeated once every six months. Instructions for obtaining a hair analysis are in the Sources section at the end of the book.

Once completed, the report will also provide other methods to remove the toxic metals from the body.

You should also be aware that there are additional triggers that can significantly impact your child's learning abilities.

Dr. John Ott is a pioneer investigator on natural and artificial light and its effect on humans, animals and plants. In his book, *Health and Light*, he shows how a neon-lit society distorts brain and nervous-system functioning. He also found that people working under pink fluorescent lights for only a few months tend to become irritable and tense. With normal fluorescent lights, students in his studies were tired, irritable, inattentive and unruly. [9] When full spectrum lights were substituted in the classroom, Dr. Ott described that the students settled down to normal. They paid more attention to their teacher, showed more interest in their studies and rarely needed discipline.

How to Correct
Mineral Deficiencies

"We must use time creatively... and forever
realize that the time is always ripe
to do right."

Martin Luther King

Children with learning disabilities are likely to be found mineral deficient in one or more minerals. Their diets tend to be imbalanced - higher in sugar, and fat, lower in protein and overall heavier in carbohydrates, pastas, etc.

Unfortunately, these imbalances may lead to many of the mineral deficiencies described in Chapter 4.

According to all known medical research, the human body needs minerals, vitamins, essential amino acids and essential fatty acids daily for optimum health. You are correct if you're imagining that you would have to eat more than your stomach could hold to get all the nutrients you need! This is true especially for foods grown on mineral deficient soil.

When you decide to supplement your child's diet with minerals, you will want the highest quality products with the best balance for your child. Oftentimes parents have told us that they have given their children mineral products, but with very inconsistent results.

There are basically three reasons for inconsistent results when taking additional mineral supplements. The first is simply an inferior or poor quality product. The second reason is that vitamin and mineral tablets contain substances to which some people are very sensitive. In their book, _Brain Allergies_, William H. Philpott, M.D. and Dwight K. Kalita, Ph.D. state that some tablets contain cornstarch as a filler; others may have sugar or food colorings in them. In milk-sensitive children, any supplement containing lactose (milk sugar) must be avoided.[1]

The third reason for inconsistent results is that people are taking forms of the minerals that cannot be as easily absorbed and utilized by the body. Before making any decisions as to which type to use for your child, it is helpful to know that there are three kinds of minerals.

The three types of minerals are: metallic, chelated and colloidal. In contrast to vitamins, minerals may not be equally available to the body in their tablet and capsule forms.

When you look at minerals in the healthfood stores you will see tablets, chelated forms and colloidal types. Metallic minerals in tablet form are the least available to the body. What typically happens is that the tablets may just travel through your body and come out whole in the waste material. Chelated minerals in capsule form are much more bioavailable and usable by the body. Chelation simply describes the process by which an amino acid, protein or enzyme is wrapped around the mineral molecule which enhances the bioavailability of the metallic mineral.

The third type of mineral is called colloidal. Colloidal chemistry isn't new, but seems to lack the medical research studies which substantiate the latest health claims. A colloid is a particle or substance that retains its identity and remains in suspension. The colloidal product information labels claim nearly perfect availability to the body.

While much research remains to be done about the effectiveness of colloidal minerals, it is true that the cultures ho live the longest (ages 120-140 years) eat plant derived colloidal minerals in their food and drink water referred to as "glacial milk" which is richest in colloidal minerals.

While we do not wish to engage in the recent medical debates about chelates vs. colloidals, we do know that many of our patients have had excellent results with both chelated and colloidal mineral forms.

For now, the research that has already been done on chelated minerals show them to be very helpful in alleviating mineral deficiencies.

We use Twinlab mineral formulas (watch the dosage for younger children) and have also used the Now brand form of colloidal minerals with good results. We have researched all of the colloidal mineral brands available, but have found only one to be consistent in its formula quality and consistent in results. We recommend that you ask your family physician before starting a mineral program for your child or follow Julian Whitaker's, M.D., information in his Health and Healing Newsletter. (See Sources section at the end of the book).

Another way to increase your child's mineral source is by adding more green vegetables, which are organically grown, to his or her diet. Other green products, commonly called the green superfoods like barley green, chlorella, algae, spirulina and wheat grass are extraordinarily helpful because they are far more potent than regular foods and are grown and harvested to miximize vitamin, mineral and amino acid concentrations. An excellent source is called Greens+

which can be found in the Sources section at the end of the book.

If you suspect that your child may be experiencing any mineral deficiencies and you decide to supplement with minerals, make sure to follow the dosage directions on the label of any mineral product you give them.

Checking Your Child's Progress

When we talk with most parents, they tell us that sometimes they feel overwhelmed when learning all this new information. Sometimes, they just do not know where to start.

So far, you may have begun to think about the relationship between what your child is eating and his or her ability to learn more easily.

Begin by imagining what would happen this week if you checked for at least one food sensitivity or tried to rotate one or two the foods in your child's diet? Write down your observations on the food log and have fun with your child when taking his or her pulse. Make it a game to encourage new eating patterns. If your child is younger and taking the pulse is too difficult, simply begin by eliminating one food that you think may be challenging to your child's health.

Begin to implement changes slowly to keep your child's progress positive and your own ability to implement the changes manageable. Decide on what changes you can make and implement a new one every week or so.

We know you will be rewarded for your efforts! And your child will begin to notice an easier time in the classroom.

Many parents have requested a supplement to the book for specific information about meal planning, food rotation and recommendations on which brand name foods to buy. In response we designed a supplement booklet called *Smart Foods, Smart Kids - Eat Your Way To Greater Brain Power Meal Planner* for parents. More information can be found in the Sources section at the end of the book.

Chapter 6

What Vitamins Do What to Which Parts?

*"When you take care of something,
it lives a long time."*

Zen Master Dainin Katagiri

Vitamins are necessary for optimum health and functioning of every system in the body. Each vitamin performs a specific task that cannot be completed by any other substance. As we mentioned earlier, the vitamins cannot do their work without the assistance of minerals. Once any mineral deficiencies are corrected however, vitamins can go to work on optimizing health.

Vitamins help achieve the manufacture of enzymes that work as catalysts, and therefore they are referred to as co-enzymes. "Except for biotin, vitamins D and K, our bodies cannot make the vitamins we need. We must provide them along with all the minerals." [1]

Drs. Lan and Wallach say in their book, *Rare Earths*, that "Vitamins regulate metabolism, facilitate the conversion of fat and carbohydrates to energy and are required for the formation and repair of tissues in embryos, children, teens, adults and seniors. Many of the solutions to preventing birth defects, reduced effectiveness during our daily lives, debilitating degenerative diseases and fatal diseases are simply to ensure an optimal intake of the essential vitamins."

Sadly, millions of Americans are poorly nourished or undernourished due to poor eating habits, processed foods and fast food consumption. This is especially true for children who are learning disabled or considered hyperactive or ADHD, according to Allan Cott, M.D.

"In 1910 only 10% of U.S. food was factory - refined or treated with artificial additives." (U.S. Department of

Agriculture.) By 1996, almost 85-90% of our foods are processed or refined in some way. Over cooking, freezing, and frying removes the necessary vitamins and nutrients from foods such as whole wheat, rice, cereal grains, vegetable oils and fruits and vegetables. The fact that the soils are so lacking in nutrients, and the pesticides and sprays further deplete the nutrients, makes our food even less available and nutritious to our children's bodies.

Dr. Cott goes on to say "...learning disabled children eat a diet which is highest in cereals and carbohydrate foods, sweets and food made with sugar. This can lead to hypoglycemia (low blood sugar) and possible diabetes. Once these foods were eliminated, children with learning disabilities and hyperactivity were treated with megavitamin therapy. The children who were treated the longest made the greatest progress."

PARENTS! We highly recommend that you begin to eliminate as sugared cereals and high fat foods from your child's diet as soon as possible.

We recommend that you use "stevia" in place of sugar, a natural sweetener with hundreds of times the potency of sugar. It is a natural herb grown in China and Brazil. It has been used for centuries in other countries, but is just becoming popular in the United States. You will have to experiment with how much will give your child the sweet taste they like. It is many times sweeter than sugar, so usually only a tiny bit will do.

Vitamin Questionnaire

The following questionnaire contains information about many vitamin deficiencies which may affect your child. By answering the questions, you will create a better picture of some deficiencies which may be affecting your child's abilities to learn. Remember that vitamins also work in tandem with the minerals. A deficiency in one area will often result in a deficiency in another.

It is not recommended that you begin giving your child individual doses of these vitamins. Some vitamins are water soluble and are not stored in the body. These include Vitamin C and the B-complex vitamins. Other vitamins are stored for longer periods of time in fatty tissue and the liver and are not water soluble. These vitamins include A, D, E, and K. Too high a dose of any non-water soluble vitamin can be toxic to the body. Both types are needed for adequate body functioning however.

A good multi vitamin *capsule* or liquid will provide the dosages that your child needs in the proper amounts. Remember that most capsules do not have binders, yeast, soy, wheat, sugars or other offending substances to which your child may be sensitive. Unfortunately, many of the children's vitamins have added colorings to make it more attractive to your child. Check with the supplemental specialist to find the brands which do not have these additives. The brands we give our families are listed at the end of this chapter.

VITAMIN A.

Does your child experience any of the following: itchy and burning eyes, light sensitivity or night blindness, loss of sense of smell, sinusitis, acne, allergies, rough and dry skin, dull dry hair, continuous infections, loss of appetite and retarded growth?   Protein cannot be used by the body without this vitamin.

We recommend only the beta carotene form of this vitamin for your child because it is converted to vitamin A in the liver.   There are many recent news reports of its cancer prevention properties also. Be aware of the dosage for your child; skin may turn yellow orange with too much of it. Be sure to read the vitamin label.

VITAMIN B-1.

Does your child experience loss of appetite, weakness, nervous irritability, hyperactivity, learning disability, memory loss, insomnia, aches and pains, mental depression, constipation, loss of weight and impaired growth?

VITAMIN B-2.

Does your child experience itching and burning of the eyes, cracking of the corners of the lips, inflammation of the mouth, purple tongue, bloodshot eyes, unhealthy skin, poor vision, fatigue and depression?

VITAMIN B-3 / NIACIN.

Does your child have rough scaly skin, diarrhea, bad breath, canker sores, hypoglycemic attacks, schizophrenia, headaches, poor memory, nausea, nervous system dysfunction, mental depression, vague aches and pains, insomnia, headaches, or loss of appetite? Is your child hyperactive?

Note: Niacin may cause a facial rash, flush or body itching. However, niacinamide can have adverse effects, especially at the high dosage. Make sure that you give your niacin only under your doctor's supervision. Melvyn Werbach, M.D. recommends that the smaller the child, the lower the dosage. He also states in his book, *Healing Through Nutrition*, that "commonly, one or both parents also need megadoses of niacin, a finding that suggests the need for abnormally high levels of niacin results from a genetic defect."

VITAMIN B-6.

This is one of the most important vitamins for the functions of the brain and for learning. According to Dr. Werbach, "Seratonin is an important neurotransmitter that may affect hyperactivity. It is derived from the amino acid tryptophan, which comes entirely from the diet. Vitamin B-6 is required to transform tryptophan to seratonin and hyperactive children with low blood levels of seratonin may respond to pyridoxine, a form of vitamin B-6. A simple blood test for seratonin can show whether a trial of the vitamin may be worthwhile."

Does your child experience nervousness, hyperactivity, allergies, joint pain and stiffness, sore mouth, depression, sensitivity to insulin, acne, convulsions, skin and nervous disorders, autoimmune and degenerative diseases, obesity, and asthma?

VITAMIN B-5 / PANTOTHENIC ACID.

Does your child experience skin abnormalities, stress, allergies, dizzy spells, digestive disturbances, retarded growth, painful or burning feet?

VITAMIN B-12.

Does your child experience pernicious anemia, fatigue, visual difficulty, anemia, difficulty walking and speaking smoothly, exhaustion, grayish color to the skin, memory loss, depression, confusion, or irritability?

BIOTIN.

Does your child experience extreme exhaustion, drowsiness, loss of appetite, anemia, muscle pains, itchy or sore skin, muscle pain, depression?

CHOLINE / INOSITOL.

Does your child experience high blood pressure, bleeding ulcers, kidney/heart troubles, loss of hair, constipation, or difficulty digesting fat?

FOLIC ACID.

Does your child experience eczema, grainy eyelids, high blood cholesterol, some forms of anemia or birth defects?

PABA.

Does your child experience energy loss, eczema, anemia, extreme fatigue?

VITAMIN C.

Does your child experience soft gums, tooth decay, loss of appetite, muscle weakness, recurring infections, anemia, skin hemorrhages, colds, poor wound healing, nosebleeds, bruising easily, bleeding gums, allergies, or frequent viral infections?

VITAMIN D.

Does your child experience tooth decay, rickets, retarded growth, muscular weakness, lack of energy, burning sensation in the mouth or throat, difficulty sleeping, difficulty seeing things far away clearly, fragile bones and teeth?

VITAMIN E.

Does your child experience cramps, dull lifeless hair, heart problems, dry skin, brittle nails, dandruff, or fatigue?

Lecithin - A Powerful Brain Booster

VITAMIN F / LECITHIN. (Unsaturated fatty acids).

Does your child experience slow or poor memory, low concentration abilities, eczema, high cholesterol, or learning disabilities? Lecithin contributes choline to the body and increases the formation of acetylcholine, a neurotransmitter. Those with learning disabilities and Alzheimer's disease are also helped with the addition of lecithin.

Lecithin is one of the most powerful brain foods known. It boosts memory and concentration powers many times over. In U.S. Government tests, lecithin has been shown to make people 25% smarter. Choline, a B vitamin, is found in lecithin, and one of the most important neurotransmitters for learning and memory is acetylcholine. The amount of acetylcholine in your brain is dependent on how much choline-rich food you eat.

Within 90 minutes of eating choline your brain boosts its memory powers, and the results last four to five hours. Imagine what would happen if children took lecithin just prior to an exam? Choline is found in egg yolks, lean beef, fish, wheat and soybeans. The strongest form of lecithin in is called phosphatidyl choline. This can be found in powdered form and stirred into juice. Once again, be sure to read dosage levels for your child on the back of the bottle. Both our families take lecithin daily.

Lecithin has also been proven to boost memory in exciting studies by the National Institute of Mental Health and the

University of Ohio as well. Dr. Richard Wurtman also recommends lecithin as a memory age-proofer. At the University of Ohio, seven of eleven Alzheimer's patients who were given lecithin showed 50 to 200 percent improvement in long-term memory. Lecithin also helps lower cholesterol in the arteries.

VITAMIN P / RUTIN / BIOFLAVINOIDS.

Does your child experience soft gums, tooth decay, loss of appetite, muscle weakness, recurring infections, anemia, skin hemorrhages, colds, poor wounds healing, nosebleeds, bruising easily, bleeding gums, allergies, or virus infections?

Although this list of vitamin needs may seem overwhelming, you may simply give your child a multiple vitamin once per day. As you look for a vitamin brand, be certain to notice whether the brand contains iron or not. Some children cannot assimilate iron and you can only determine this by asking your doctor. You will also want to give your child capsules or liquid for better absorption.

We use a brand called Daily One Caps by Twinlab or if your child prefers a powder, dissolved in juice, All One Brand makes a powder form. If you have a younger child, find a children's vitamin formula in the liquid form, being careful to avoid colorings, flavorings and preservatives. We do not recommend any of the chewable types of vitamins due to the additives which may cause problems for children who are sensitive. Vitamin potency is affected sunlight. Be sure to store them in the dark containers they came in.

Chapter 7

Brilliant Brain Foods

How Amino Acids Make Your Child Smarter

*"Man's mind stretched to a new idea
never goes back to its original dimensions."*

Oliver Wendell Holmes

Neurotransmitters - Brain Talk

Remember Brandon in Chapter 1? Once the adjustments were made in his diet, and vitamin/mineral supplements added, his mother reported even more outstanding results when amino acids were added to his daily regimen. She told us that his concentration and behavior improved dramatically. Medical research tells us that higher levels of concentration and memory are specifically connected to increased levels of certain neurotransmitters in the brain.

A neurotransmitter is a chemical made of protein that allows brain cells to communicate with one another. Neurotransmitters determine your mental and emotional state of well being. Although there are about 50 neurotransmitters in your brain, only about 10 carry on the communication between the cells.

You can think of a neurotransmitter like a runner who lights the torch of the next runner for the Olympic games. Each runner, in turn, does the same and then falls back. If a brain cell is stimulated it releases a neurotransmitter which carries a message to the next cell. This continues along the thousands of neural pathways in the brain and happens within a split second.

Some neurotransmitters order voluntary muscle movement, some carry sensations of pain, while others carry excitatory and inhibitory emotional responses. Whatever you react to, whether you are happy, amused or depressed, all depends on the chemical language of the brain. So when your child is acting out, feeling depressed or behaving in a hyperactive or hyper-passive way, it is all governed by the neurotransmitters in the brain. Too many of them or too few will cause over or under reactions to a stimulus.

It is important to understand that every cell in the human body is controlled by the brain. If these cells are not nourished properly, what you will see is illness in some form, disease, improper behavior or inability to concentrate, learn and remember.

If your child has a neurotransmitter problem, drugs cannot address the root of the problem. All a drug such as Ritalin or Dexedrine can do is stimulate temporary excessive release of preexisting neurotransmitter stores. Drugs will not increase production of neurotransmitters. This is why the drugs will often lose their effect over periods of long term use. Once the preexisting neurotransmitter stores are exhausted, the drug is not able to stimulate further neurotransmitter release into the synapses between the neurons. That is why you will hear of a drug abuse "crash" which occurs frequently.

If optimal levels of neurotransmitters existed in the brain we would not be seeing epidemic levels of anti-depressants, anti-manic, anti-schizophrenic and Attention Deficit Disorder drugs being prescribed. Drugs do not produce or increase production of neurotransmitters, they are only addressing the symptoms and not the causes of the problem.

The only thing that can actually increase the production of neurotransmitters is proper nutrition. There are billions of neurons or brain cells which must be fed continually. They require amino acids, vitamins, minerals, oxygen and fatty acids. These nutrients travel to the brain by way of the bloodstream. Billie J. Sahley, Ph.D., author of *Healing With Amino Acids*,[1] says, "The brain feeds on energy in the form of a chemical called ATP (adenosine triphoshate). This energy is the fuel to generate neurotransmitters (the chemical language of the brain), conduct electrical impulses, transport proteins throughout the cells, extend new nerve connections to other brain cells and rebuild worn-out cell membranes."

"The brain must create its own energy for the billions of neurons that it must feed. It cannot borrow or steal this energy from other parts of the body." In order to make this energy, the brain must be fed the proper nourishment. Since the brain burns only glucose under normal, non-fasting conditions, it cannot store sugar in its cells and it depends on second by second fuel delivery by the blood circulating through the brain.

Feeding Your Child's Brain

What then is the proper nourishment for your child's brain (and your own)? Along with the vitamins, colloidal minerals and essential fatty acids discussed earlier, amino acids in particular, along with lecithin, are extraordinary brain power and mental clarity boosters, as well as memory and concentration enhancers. Amino acids have been medically proven to raise I.Q. scores and calm hyperactivity as well. All major neurotransmitters are made from amino acids and from dietary protein. Even when vitamins and minerals are absorbed properly they will not be effective unless amino acids are present.

Amino acids are the building blocks of protein. Protein is essential to life because it provides the structure for all living things. It is imperative for the growth of bones and it makes up the muscles, ligaments, tendons, glands, organs, hair, nails and body fluids (except for urine and bile).

Dr. Billie Sahley says that everything from the neurotransmitters to the protein your body uses to run and rebuild itself are created from singular, isolated amino acids. The central nervous system cannot even function without amino acids which act as neurotransmitters or as precursors to the neurotransmitters. And protein cannot exist or be complete without all of its particular amino acids.

There are 29 known amino acids which form over 1600 basic proteins. These basic proteins make up over 75% of the body's solid weight.

Our bodies require at least "20 times as much in amino acids intake as it does for vitamins, and about 4 times as much as minerals," says Billie Jay Sahley, Ph.D., author of _The Anxiety Epidemic_ and _The Natural Way to Control Hyperactivity._[2,3]

The liver produces about 80% of all needed amino acids and the remaining 20% must be obtained from our food. However, poor diet and pollutants mean that the **"essential amino acids"** (those which the body cannot make on its own) are not often sufficient to allow the body to make its own (**"non-essential"**) amino acids.

If the essential amino acids are not all present at the same time and in specific proportion, the other amino acids cannot be used for metabolizing protein. In children with "learning disabilities", the messages in the brain are not reaching the proper receptor sites because there is a shortage of neurotransmitters. Since neurotransmitters are responsible for learning and behavior, a deficiency will have a dramatic effect on your child's ability to learn. Without the added help of amino acids your child will not automatically manufacture more neurotransmitters. Amino acids will not only restore the proper balance of these neurotransmitters, they will help create new ones.

In addition, there has been much research to show skyrocketing I.Q. scores when patients are given amino acids as part of their nutritional program.

Any mental or physical activity will cause your brain cells to release neurotransmitters which they use to communicate with one another. Excellent memory and boosted learning power are connected with high levels of specific neurotransmitters. Dr. Richard Wurtman of MIT made the discovery that what you eat determines how many and how much of these neurotransmitters your brain makes.   Dr. Wurtman, editor of "*Nutrition and the Brain*", says that "The brain is not above it all. It is intimately influenced by what we eat."

Research at MIT showed that brain transmitter levels could be significantly influenced by a high protein meal. A high protein meal will result in high adrenaline/norepinephrine levels which create higher levels of alertness.

If your child is under any type of stress, whether in school, at home or on the playing field, the brain's need for amino acids is increased. In his book, *Prescription for Nutritional Healing*, James Balch, M.D. notes that, "The process of assembling amino acids to make proteins or breaking down proteins into individual amino acids for the body's use is continuous... Should the body deplete itself of its reserves of any of the essential amino acids, it would not be able to produce those proteins requiring such amino acids. The resulting protein shortage could easily lead to a number of disorders." For example, children with brain damage such as Down's syndrome, require much higher quantities of amino acids than other children.

Following is a list of the main amino acids and their functions. When you choose to supplement your child's diet with amino acids, be certain to check labels of either liquid or capsule forms and notice the dosage and proportions. Simply giving one or two amino acids or large amounts of single amino acids is not appropriate for your child and may do more harm than good. Megadosing does not restore brain chemistry. Balance is the key to regulating brain chemistry.

In the Sources section you will find amino acids that are in the proper balanced formula for your child and yourself. Greens+ and Twinlab have a complete amino acid formula as do several other companies.

Additionally, Dr. Sahley lists several products in her books on amino acids from The Pain and Stress Center in San Antonio Texas. There are formulas of amino acids, vitamins and minerals that are perfect for children with learning disabilities. Call their clinic at 1 (800) 669-CALM for more information.

It is also advisable to check with your physician or health care practitioner about performing an amino acid analysis prior to beginning any amino acid supplementation.

When you do take amino acids, be sure to take them on an empty stomach because they compete for entry into the brain. Following is a list of the amino acids - essential and non-essential.

Remember - essential amino acids are those the body cannot manufacture and non-essential are formed by metabolic activity in the body. Also, vitamin B6 is needed to allow assimilation of amino acids.

Alanine (non-essential)

This helps the blood glucose levels, especially as an energy storage source for the muscles and liver. It activates muscles and boosts the immune system.

Arginine (semi-essential)

This is a fundamental stimulant for growth hormone and immune response in the liver and pituitary. It increases muscle tone while decreasing fat. It also helps heal wounds and blocks formation of tumors.

Arginine curbs the appetite and aids in metabolizing fats for weight loss. If the herpes simplex virus is present keep the amount of arginine low and increase lysine. If the herpes virus is present in the body, it can be helped by eliminating foods with arginine such as peanut butter, nuts, and cheese.

Aspartic Acid (non-essential)

This is found in beets and sugar cane and is used mainly as a sweetener. As a precursor of threonine, it is a neurotransmitter made with ATP that increases the body's resistance to fatigue. Aspartic acid has a protective function over the liver and promotes mineral uptake in the intestinal tract. It helps to make healthy DNA.

Branch Chain Amino Acids (essential)

These are leucine, isoleucine and valine (BCAA's). They are called the stress amino acids and must be taken in correct proportion. They aid in hemoglobin formation, help stabilize blood sugar and reduce high blood sugar levels. Leucine helps reduce hypoglycemic symptoms.

Carnitine (non-essential)

This amino acid helps regulate fat metabolism through enzyme stimulation. It speeds fat oxidation for weight loss and helps eliminate excess triglycerides in the blood. It also helps prostaglandin metabolism. Carnitine helps children with diabetes because it decreases ketone levels.

Cysteine (semi-essential)

This works as an antioxidant to protect against radiation toxicity and free radical damage to skin and arteries. It works to promote red and white blood cell reproduction and tissue restoration in lung diseases. If it is taken with evening primrose oil, cysteine protects the brain and body from alcohol and tobacco effects. Cysteine must be used with caution in diabetics due to changes in the insulin cycle.

Cystine (semi-essential)

This is the oxidized form of cysteine, and it promotes white blood cell activity and healing of burns and wounds. Cystine is the main ingredient of hair and it is essential to the formation of skin.

Calming Hyperactive Kids

There is an amino acid called GABA - Gamma Amino Butyric Acid (an inhibitory neurotransmitter) which has the ability to actually mimic the tranquilizing effect of Librium and Valium, but without the sedation effect. It reduces anxiety by decreasing limbic firing.

Thousands of documents and texts on GABA describe exactly how it affects stress and anxiety in the brain due to the fact that it crosses the blood/brain barrier.

If your child is particularly hyperactive, and you have already removed all the triggers from his or her diet, GABA may be your answer to a calmer household and a calmer child. A hyperactive child has anxiety which gets stored in the limbic system (emotional system) of the brain.

When that stress/anxiety is prolonged, the limbic system releases so many anxiety-related messages that the child becomes overwhelmed and either hyper-aggressive or hyper-passive. Then, the child actually cannot control his or her behavior or make good decisions.

When you wonder why your child cannot seem to make good choices in certain situations, he or she may actually have empty GABA receptors in the brain. In the Sources Section, you will find amino acids made especially for children with learning disabilities (as well as some for yourself!).

Caution! GABA works well in partnership with Vitamin B6. Do not use the GABA that has anything else with it like niacinamide or inositol - there can be undesirable effects.

Glutamic Acid (non-essential)

Over 50% of the amino acid composition of the brain is glutamic acid and its derivatives. It is a critical fuel for the brain because it transports potassium across the blood/brain barrier.

At Columbia College of Physicians and Surgeons, retarded children given glutamic acid, a true brain fuel, gained 11 to 17 I.Q. points! Dr. Abram Hoffer, a father of Orthomolecular medicine, used L-glutamine to overcome mental retardation, senility and schizophrenia. L-glutamine also decreases the body's cravings for sweets and alcohol.

Glutamine (non-essential)

This is one of the best nutrients for the brain. It is most plentiful and provides an alternative food source for the brain when blood sugar levels are low. It improves memory retention, concentration, recall and alertness. Glutamine also reduces sugar and alcohol cravings and controls hypoglycemic reactions.

Glutamine is also a precursor for GABA which is especially powerful as a concentration aid for children with ADD.

Glutathione (non-essential)

This helps neutralize radiation toxicity and inhibit free radicals. It also helps white blood cells kill bacteria. Glutathione helps remove heavy metal pollutants also.

Glycine (non-essential)

Glycine is an amino acid used for psychiatric disorders and in reducing aggression. It is an inhibitory neurotransmitter. It is also used as a sugar substitute because of its sweet taste. Glycine is also helpful in removing lead from the body.

There are many other amino acids which actually create a "smarter" brain. See Sources for specific references. We highly recommend free form amino acids for parents and teachers as well.

Histidine (essential)

This is an essential amino acid for infants, not adults. It helps relieve the pain of rheumatoid arthritis and always needs to be taken with Vitamin C (ester -c). It helps chelate toxic metals from the body and is necessary for the proper functioning of the auditory nerves. Use with caution in women prone to depression due to P.M.S.

Lysine (essential)

Lysine is found in muscle, connective tissue and collagen. It is needed for proper growth and bone development in children. One of its many benefits is that it inhibits growth and replication of the herpes and Epstein Barr viruses. It is especially important for those recovering from surgery, because it helps build muscle protein.

If a person is deficient in lysine, he or she experiences a loss of energy, inability to concentrate, bloodshot eyes, anemia and hair loss.

Methionine (essential)

This amino acid supports healthy skin and nails and prevents hair loss. It acts as an anti-oxidant and free radical deactivator and is especially helpful against chemical allergic reactions.

Ornithine (non-essential)

Ornithine helps metabolize excess body fat when combined with arginine and carnitine. It stimulates growth hormone production and may be useful in autoimmune diseases.

Phenylalanine (essential)

Another amino acid brain booster is called phenylalanine. It produces neurotransmitters and is used by your brain in manufacturing epinephrine which is very important in memory, learning and concentration. It also relieves depression and stress. Phenylalanine is available in all protein foods or in capsules at the health food store. Remember, a lack of concentration and memory loss in your child may also be a result of low levels of depression. We know of many psychiatrists who treat ADD/ADHD with antidepressants. If you can create a natural antidepressant, without the side effects of drugs, phenylalanine may well deserve a try.

Phenylalanine also comes in another form called DLPA which is the building block of all amino acids. Both forms used together create energy, higher mental abilities, creativity, better concentration and also relieve pain and depression. They are especially good for pain control. Many children diagnosed with ADD/ADHD have a higher incidence of turning to drug abuse to create the feelings they want. Phenylalanine and DLPA together will naturally boost their mental abilities and relieve depression naturally without any negative effect.

Do not use phenylalanine if you are pregnant, diabetic or have high blood pressure. It also should not be taken with MAO and tricyclic antidepressants, and when melanoma is present.

Proline (semi-essential)

This amino acid is helpful in lowering blood pressure and improving skin texture by aiding in the production of collagen. Take with Vitamin C.

Taurine (non-essential)

Taurine is a neurotransmitter that helps control hyperactivity and nervous system imbalance. It also normalizes irregular heartbeat. In order for the central nervous system to function properly, taurine is needed. Many studies have shown it to be especially effective in calming hyperactive or hyperkinetic movements.

Epilepsy, anxiety, hyperactivity and poor brain function are related to taurine deficiency.

Threonine (essential)

This helps maintain proper protein balance in the body and increases glycine levels in the brain. It also helps control epileptic seizures and prevents accumulation of fat in the liver.

Tryptophan (essential)

Tryptophan is necessary for the production of niacin and is used by the brain to produce serotonin, a necessary neurotransmitter. It helps to control hyperactivity, relieves stress and enhances the release of growth hormone. It acts as a mood stabilizer, calming aggression and obsessive behavior. This must be taken with vitamin B-6 to be effective.

Dr. Balch's book, *Prescription for Nutritional Healing*, states that "The Center for Disease Control established an association between a rare blood disorder (EMS) and tryptophan and the FDA has since recalled all products in which tryptophan is the sole or major component. However, the cause of EMS is still unknown." Unfortunately, it was only one contaminated batch of tryptophan that had been made by a Japanese firm, Showa Denko, which caused a health problem. Even though the problem was corrected, and the CDC has released tryptophan, the FDA has not. Tryptophan was used successfully by millions of people for over 40 years.

Tyrosine (non-essential)

In U.S. Army and Harvard Medical School tests, another amino acid, L-tyrosine, has been proven to help people cope with mega stress, relieve depression and boost mental abilities. Alan Gelenberg, M.D., Department of Psychiatry at Harvard Medical School, found tyrosine to be more effective than antidepressants.

Tyrosine acts as a mood elevator, suppresses the appetite and reduces body fat. Tyrosine aids in the production of melanin and in the functions if the adrenal, thyroid and pituitary glands. If it is deficient, it triggers a deficiency of the hormone, norephinephrine, at a specific brain location.

Tyrosine should not be taken with MAO and tricyclic antidepressants or when cancerous melanoma is present.

Vitamin B6 and magnesium are essential to the assimilation of all amino acids. Yet, when food is processed it depletes over 75% of the magnesium.

Research on amino acids provide exciting new developments into increasing brain power. Dr. Richard Wurtman of MIT says that "the brain's ability to make certain neurotransmitters depends on the amount of various nutrients circulating in the blood." One of the ways to increase these nutrients is with amino acids.

To the reader:

Many new developments are pending in the health field.

If you are interested in more information and new legislation, there is a non-profit consumer organization which has up-to-date information.

If you would like more information, please write or call:

Citizens for Health
Natural Activist Newsletter
P.O. Box 2260
Boulder, CO 80306

Telephone: 1 (800) 357-2211 or (303) 417-0772

A subscription costs $25.00 and includes membership in their organization. You can also receive a subscription to National Fax Network for important updates in the health field for an additional fee.

Chapter 8

Parent Planner Summary and More Natural Remedies

"Nothing splendid has ever been achieved except by those who dared believe that something inside of them was superior to circumstance."

Bruce Barton

This chapter can be used as your Planner for getting started and will give you an overview of the information you have just read. You will also find a list of other natural remedies.

1. Educate Yourself on Food Ingredients

To begin with, parents need to educate themselves and their children on food ingredients. Read the labels and become familiar with the ingredients in packaged and canned goods. The best advice is, if you can't pronounce it, don't eat it! Also, there are numerous books available at your local health food store to help you decipher these ingredients and what they mean. Also, read books on fast food facts so you know exactly what is in them and whether they are healthy for your child.

2. Keep a Food Journal

Have you and your child keep a journal of what is eaten and how he or she reacts to the chemicals, additives and food colorings in the foods eaten daily. Remember, the average child gets about 1/4 to 1/3 of his daily calories from snacks. Observe your child carefully and use the meal planner described on page 97 to help plan meals and rotate foods.

In your journal, check off the following symptoms and conditions of allergies to these chemicals and additives:

a.   Appearance and skin - pale skin (white or ghostly looking), dark circles under the eyes, puffy eyes, hives, itchy skin, red skin, eczema (itchy, flaking dry skin), skin eruptions and canker sores.

b.   Respiratory/nasal - Runny nose, congestion, coughing, hay fever, sinus, stuffy nose, wheezing, sneezing, itching, discharge, post-nasal drip, mouth breathing, asthma, nose bleeds, frequent colds.

c.   Urological - Bed wetting, frequent and painful urination.

d.   Gastrointestinal - Diarrhea, gas, bloating, indigestion, stomach aches, constipation, cramping, vomiting, heartburn, nausea.

e.   Cardiovascular - Irregular heartbeat, rapid pulse, high or low blood pressure.

f.   Ear Conditions - Loss of hearing, ear aches, frequent ear infections.

g.   Eye Conditions - Blurred vision, tearing, sensitivity to light, eye pain and conjunctivitis, itching, feeling heavy, double vision, spots, decreased acuity.

8.   Muscular-skeletal - Arthritis, frequent muscle pains and aches not typical growing pains, muscle spasms, painful joints, swelling, weakness and cramps.

h.   Other types of signs - very strong body odor, excessive sweating, night sweats, under or overweight, frequent virus infections, low blood sugar.   Observe if your child becomes dizzy, fatigued, or falls asleep.   You also will want to watch for stimulated types of behavior like acting silly, intoxicated, hyperactivity, anxiety, fear, panic, irritation or anger.

i.   Mental behavior - Depressions, drowsiness, general fatigue, insomnia, irritability, nervousness, hyperactivity, poor concentration, poor memory, restlessness, learning disabilities not due to brain trauma, anxiety, floating sensations, poor muscle coordination, sleeping at inappropriate times.

j.   Learning problems - poor reading comprehension, poor concentration, memory loss, slurred speech, stammering, stuttering, math and spelling errors, inability to be attentive. Although your child may have previously experienced these symptoms, what you will be looking for is an increase in the intensity level due to the allergic response.

Once you carefully observe the types of reactions your child is having, you can easily test for specific food allergies without expensive medical testing. You can do this by the following pulse test method:

3. Take The Pulse Test for Food Allergies

See chapter 3 for instructions on Dr. Coca's pulse test for food allergies.

4. Supplement with vitamin "capsules", amino acids and lecithin

If your child is old enough, use capsules and not tablets. Remember that tablets are not as easily absorbed by the body. You may also empty the capsules into unsweetened applesauce. Include amino acids and lecithin for increasing your child's brain power and mental health. As you read in Chapter 6, Twinlab has a good we use called "Daily One" (with and without iron) and if you have a younger child, you might want to try one of the powdered or liquid vitamin forms. Check with the supplement specialist at your health food store, as well as your physician if your child is an infant.

In his booklet, *Hyperactivity and the Attention Deficit Disorder*, William Crook, M.D., suggests that you give daily doses of yeast free vitamins and evening primrose oil. He also recommends that you use only oils that are unrefined like olive oil and flaxseed oil. We have found the "Now" brand to be a good source for evening primrose oil. Although it does not mention it on the label, refrigeration extends the life of the product. "My teenage children take one of these per day", says co-author Pat Wyman. If your child is younger, get a capsule with a lesser dosage.

5. Give liquid colloidal minerals or minerals in capsules

6. Obtain a hair analysis

This will determine whether or not your child has mineral deficiencies or toxic metal concentrations in his or her system. If the hair analysis confirms toxic metals, use the cleansing formula listed in chapter 2 (or the formula sent in the results packet) to help eliminate the toxins from your child's body. (See Sources for how to obtain a hair analysis).

7. Control Your Child's Environment

It is important for your child's health to keep his or her environment as pure as possible. Remove tobacco smoke and any environmental chemicals (such as CFC's, nail polish, formaldehyde in foam pillows and mattresses, asbestos, household chemicals, perfumes, insecticides, and chlorine bleach).

8. Help Your Child Succeed in School

Teach your child how to become "school smart" by using optimum learning strategies which match learning and testing styles. Your child will want to learn for a lifetime if he or she knows "how to learn." Spend time at school with your child's teachers and ask what adjustments can be made to the assignments that are more suitable to the way your child learns. (See Sources).

9. Give Your Child Mental "Hugs"

Many children need additional doses of support and encouragement. Some of the things you can do to help make raising your child easier are:

a. Smile more often - try to maintain a sense of humor about your parenting skills and your child's needs as well.

b. Notice and praise your child when he or she is doing something right.

c. Give simple tasks one at a time. Most children with learning challenges become overwhelmed when given too many directions at once. Make sure that your child repeats the directions to you so that you know they were heard.

d. Be consistent with rewards and rules.

e. Partner with your child when making rules and their consequences. Include him or her in the entire process.

f. Listen to your child and make him or her feel that you care about what he needs and wants.

10. Read and gain more information on other natural therapies

Reports in national magazines like Time and Newsweek indicate that many parents report excellent results with natural remedies such as chiropractic, acupuncture, massage, flower remedies, a substance called pycnogenol, Essiac tea, homeopathic remedies, biofeedback training, super blue-green algae, edukinesthetics, herbal therapy, mind-body medicine, sound therapy, etc. The book, *Alternative Medicine*, is an excellent and comprehensive reference for each of these remedies. If you are especially interested in herbal remedies, we recently found a very informative Internet website at http://www.drherbs.com.

One outstanding (and great tasting) product that we have used to nourish and balance the body is called Greens+. This product is made from the purest organically grown ingredients and offers children a perfectly balanced amino acid profile and nutrients that they need. Research done by Dr. Linus Pauling and adolescent physchologist, biochemist Sam Graci, show that many learning disability symptoms are nutritionally based and Greens+ is an excellent answer to alleviating these learning disability symptoms. It can be mixed with water or juice and easily given to children with no history of sensitivities to any of the ingredients.

Greens+ is winner of the NNFA Product of the Year Award in the Beverage category; National Product of the Year from the International Hall of Fame; and Product of the Year in Canada. It is also listed in Harvey Diamond's new book, *You Can Prevent Breast Cancer* and used by David Letterman to enhance his health.

Greens+ can be obtained at many health food stores or by calling the Orange Peel Company at 1 (800) 643-1210. In Canada, the company is at 1 (800) 258-0444.

Sources

1. Meal Planner

The Smart Foods, Smart Kids - Meal Planner for Parents and Kids is available from The Center for New Discoveries in Learning. Call 1 (707) 837-8180.

2. Hair Analysis

To obtain a complete hair analysis and nutritional correction report, send a self-addressed stamped envelope for a questionnaire to: Dr. Sandra Hills, c/o The Center for New Discoveries in Learning, P.O. Box 1019, Windsor, CA 95492.

3. Vitamins and colloidal minerals

We use the Twinlab vitamin products and the Now Brand colloidal mineral products. Colloidal minerals can be obtained in the health food stores, and be sure to watch the dosage for younger children. The "Now" brand has a colloidal mineral product which does not contain sugar.

4. High Quality Vitamins and Minerals by Mail Order

The Life Extension Foundation is non-profit organization which has an outstanding line of the finest vitamins, minerals and supplements available. The are a research organization and understand your child's special needs. They are at 1 (800) 544-4440. Call them for a mail order catalog.

5. Amino Acids

Greens+ has a perfectly balanced amino acid profile and can be dissolved in juice or water. Call 1 (800) 643-1210 or ask for it in your health food store. In Canada call 1 (800) 258-0444. Your child will love it!

6. For Medical Help, Diagnosis and Monthly Newsletter

Julian Whitaker, M.D., directs the Whitaker Wellness Institute in Newport Beach, CA. You may contact them directly for medical help, diagnosis and treatment for your child. Dr. Whitaker is also the author of the world renowned newsletter known as *Health and Healing* and one we consider to be a **must-read** for you and your family. Dr. Whitaker has recently researched and written a great deal on help for children with Downs Syndrome. You may contact Dr. Whitaker and subscribe to his newsletter at 1 (800) 777-5015.

7. Learning Strategies for your child - Learn How To Learn

Children with learning differences like ADHD benefit from specific types of learning strategies that help them match learning and testing styles for greater success in school. The non-profit Center for New Discoveries in Learning offers a *School Smart Kids* newsletter, *Super Speller Strategy* video which guarantees spelling success, *Super Teaching Strategies* learning videos, and *Gift of Dyslexia*, video course for dyslexia correction. They also offer self-esteem and accelerated learning products to help your child be successful in school. All subject areas are included and have been proven successful with over 40,000 students. Each strategy has been shown to raise CTBS (national testing) scores between 12 and 15 percentile points. Please see their Website at http://www.howtolearn.com or contact them at 1 (707) 837-8180.

8. For learning math facts

The Teaching Company's *"I'm Smart, I Taught Myself the Times Tables"*, by Joy Ridenour. This is a wonderful book, with audio tapes included to help your child learn their facts easily and quickly. There is an English and a Spanish language edition available. Please see http://www.howtolearn.com for ordering information or call 1 (707) 837-8180.

8. To improve reading abilities and strengthen visual skills

If your child is experiencing vision/perceptual difficulties as he or she reads, we recommend that you read *A+ Vision* Book by Drs. Beth and Greg Gilman. It contains hundreds of fun and easy to do eye exercises to help your child read more efficiently and smoothly. The entire book is reproducible. See http://www.howtolearn.com for more information or call 1 (707) 837-8180.

For Dyslexia Correction Training contact the Reading Research Council in Burlingame, CA at 1 (415) 692-8990.

9. For Making Behavioral Changes

Contact Powerlearning Corporation for information and seminars about helping your child to make behavioral changes. Donald Lofland, Ph.D. is the author of Powerlearning and Thought Viruses. Call 1 (408) 425-7971.

Recommended Readings:

1. Balch, P. And Balch, J. *Rx Dietary Wellness*, Greenfield, IN:PAB Publishing, 1992.
2. Bland, Jeffrey. *Bioflavonoids*.   New Canaan, CT: Keats Publishing Company, 1994.
3. Block, Mary Ann, *No More Ritalin, Treating ADHD Without Drugs*, New York: Kensington Books, 1996.
4. Braly, J. *Dr. Braley's Food Allergy and Nutrition Revolution*, New Canaan, CT: Keats Publishing Company, 1992.
5. Brostoff J., and Gamlin, L. *The Complete Guide to Food Allergy and Intolerance*.   London: Bloomsbury Publishing, Ltd., 1989.
6. The Burton Goldberg Group, *Alternative Medicine -The Definitive Guide*. Puyallup, WA: Future Medicine Publishing, Inc., 1993.
7. Carper, J. *Stop Aging Now*.   New York: Harper Collins, 1995.
8. Cott, A. *Megavitamins*: *The Orthomolecular Approach*.   San Rafael: Academic Press, 1972.
9. Crook, William. *Chronic Fatigue Syndrome and the Yeast Connection*. Jackson, TN: Professional Books, 1992.
10. Crook, William. *The Yeast Connection Handbook*. Tennessee: Professional Books, 1996.
11. Crook, William. *Help For The Hyperactive Child - A Good Sense Guide for Parents*. Tennessee: Professional Books, 1991.
12. Crook, William. *Tracking Down Hidden Food Allergy*. Tennessee: Professional Books, 1978.
13. Crook, W.G. and Jones, M.H. *The Yeast Connection Cookbook*. Jackson, TN: Professional Books, 1989.
14. Davis, Adelle, Ph.D. *Let's Get Well*. New York: Harcourt Brace and Company, 1975.
15. Davis, Ronald. *The Gift of Dyslexia*. New York: Perigee Books, 1997.

16. Dennison, Paul and Gail. *Brain Gym, Brain Gym Teachers Edition.* Ventura, CA: Edu-Kinesthetics, 1986, 1989, 1994.

17. DePorter, Bobbi. *Quantum Learning.* New York: Dell Trade, 1992.

18. Faelten, S. *The Allergy Self-Help Book.* Emmaus, Penn.: Rodale Press, 1983.

19. Franz, Marion J. *Fast Food Facts.* Minneapolis: Chronimed Publications, 1994.

20. Fredericks, Carlton, Ph.D. *Low Blood Sugar and You.* New York: Grosset and Dunlap, 1970.

21. Golick, M. "She Thought I was Dumb: But I Told Her I Had a Learning Disability." Quebec Association for Children With Learning Disabilities.

22. Hartmann, Thom. *Attention Deficit Disorder: A Different Perception.* Grass Valley, CA: Underwood Books, 1993.

23. Haas, E.M. Staying Healthy With Nutrition. Berkeley, CA: Celestial Arts, 1992.

24. Heimlich, J. *What Your doctor Won't Tell You -Alternative Therapies.* New York:Harper Collins, 1990.

25. Holt, John. *How Children Fail.* New York: Dell Publishing Co., 1964.

26. Hoffer, Abram, Ph.D., M.D. *Orthomolecular Nutrition.* New Canaan, Conn., Keats Publishing, Inc. 1978.

27. Hunter, Beatric Trum. *Consumer Beware.* New York: Bantam Books, Inc., 1972.

28. Jacobson, M.F. and Maxwell, B. *What Are We Feeding Our Kids?* New York: Workman Publishing Company, 1994.

29. Karschmann, John D. *Nutrition Almanac.* New York: McGraw-Hill, 1996.

30. Levy, Harold B. *Square Pegs, Round Holes.* New York: Little Brown and Company, 1973.

31. Lofland, Donald, Ph.D. *Powerlearning.* Stamford, CT: Longmeadow Press: 1992.

32. Lofland, Donald, Ph.D.   *Thought Viruses*. New York: Harmony Press, 1997.

33. Mendelsohn, Robert S.   *How To Raise A Healthy Child*. Chicago: Contemporary Books, Inc., 1984.

34. Oski, F. *Don't Drink Your Milk - Facts about the world's most overrated nutrient* -Ninth Edition.   New York: Teach Services, 1992.

35. Pfeiffer, Carl, M.D.   *Mental and Elemental Nutrients*. New Canaan, Conn.: Keats Publishing, 1975.

36. Philpott, William H., M.D., and Kalita, Ph.D.   *Brain Allergies*. New Canaan, Conn.: Keats Publishing, 1980.

37. Randolph, T. G.   *Human Ecology and Susceptibility to the Chemical Environment*.   Springfield, Ill.:   Charles Thomas Publishers, 1976.

38. Randolph, T. G.   "Allergy, A Cause of Fatigue, Irritability and Behavior Problems of Children". J. Of Pediatrics, 31:560, 1947.

39. Rapp, Doris.   *Is This Your Child*?   New York: Bantam Doubleday, 1996.

40. Robbins, John. *Reclaiming Our Health*. Tiburon, CA: H.J. Kramer, 1996.

41. Robbins, John.   *Diet for a New America*.   Walpole, NH: Stillpoint, 1987.

42. Rowe, A. H.   "Allergic Toxemia and Migraine Due to Food Allergy." California and Western Medicine. 33:785, 1930.

43. Rowe, A. H. *Food Allergy*: *Its Manifestation and Control on The Elimination Diet*. Springfield, Ill.: Charles C. Thomas Publishers, 1972.

44. Siguel, E.N. *Essential Fatty Acids in Health and Disease*. *Brookline*, MA: Nutrek Press, 1994.

45. Smith, L.M. *Feed Your Body Right*. New York: M. Evans, 1994.

46. Valett, R. *Modifying Children's Behavior.* From CANHC, California Association of Neurologically Handicapped Children Distribution Center, P. O. Box 1526, Vista, Ca., 92083.
47. Weil, A.T., *Spontaneous Healing.* New York: Knopf, 1995.
48. Werbach, M. *Healing Through Nutrition.* New York: Harper Collins, 1993.

Index

Bibliography

Chapter 1 - What's Food Got to Do With It?
[1] Crook, William. *Hyperactivity and the Attention Deficit Disorder*, Jackson, Tenn: Professional Books, 1995.

Chapter 2 - From Food To Mood
[1] Mandell, Marshall. *5 Day Allergy Relief System.* New York: Thomas Y. Crowell, 1979.
[2] Werbach, Melvyn., M.D. *Healing Through Nutrition.*, New York: Harper Collins, 1993.
[3] Hoffer, Abram. *Orthomolecular Nutrition.* New Canaan, Conn.: Keats Publishing, Inc., 1978.
[4] Schoenthaler, S.J. "The Impact of a Low Food Additive and Sucrose Diet on Academic Performance in 803 New York City Public Schools". Int J Biosocial Res 8(2):185-95, 1986.
[5] Philpott, William H. *Brain Allergies - The Psychonutrient Connection.* New Canaan: Conn. Keats Publishing Co., Inc., 1980.
[6] Hoffer, Abram. *Orthomolecular Nutrition.* New Canaan, Conn.: Keats Publishing, Inc., 1978.
[7] Hippchen, Leonard J. *Ecologic-Biochemical Approaches to Treatment of Delinquents and Criminals.* London: Vannostrand, Reinhold Company, 1978.
[8] Werbach, Melvyn., M.D. *Healing Through Nutrition.*, New York: Harper Collins, 1993.
[9] Carper, Jean. *Stop Aging Now!* New York: Harper Collins, 1995.
[10] Crook, William. *Hyperactivity and the Attention Deficit Disorder.* Jackson, Tenn: Professional Books, 1995.

Chapter 3. The Coca Pulse Test for Food Allergies
[1] Coca, Arthur, F. *The Pulse Test, Easy Allergy Detection.* New York: Harper Collins, 1996.

Chapter 4. The Hidden Triggers
[1] Lan, Ma and Wallach, J. D. *Let's Play Doctor.* Bonita, CA: Double Happiness Publishing Co., 1989.

[2] Feingold, Benjamin. *Why Your Child is Hyperactive*. New York: Random House, 1974.

[3] Powers, Hugh. "Dietary Measures to Improve Behavior and Achievement". Academic Therapy 9:3, 1973.

[4] Werbach, Melvyn., M.D. *Healing Through Nutrition.*, New York: Harper Collins, 1993.

[5] Shapiro, H. A. "Arsenic Content of Human Hair and Nails: Its Interpretation", J of Forensic Med. 14:65-71, 1967.

[6] Thatcher, R. W., Lester, M. L. "Nutrition, Environmental Toxins and Computerized EEG: A Mini-Max Approach to Learning Disabilities," J. Learn Disabilities 18(5):287-97, 1985.

[7] Needleman, H. L., Gatsonis, C. A. "Low-Level Lead Exposure and the I.Q. of Children. A Meta Analysis of Modern Studies. JAMA 263(5):673-8, 1990.

[8] Rees, Elizabeth, L., "Aluminum Toxicity As Indicated by Hair Analysis," Reprint in the Journal of Orthomolecular Psychiatry, Vol. 8, No. 1, 1975.

[9] Ott, John. *Health and Light*. Greenwich, Conn.: Devin Adair Publishers, 1988.

Chapter 5. How To Correct Mineral Deficiencies

[1] Philpott, William H. and Kalita, Dwight, M. C. *Brain Allergies*. New Canaan, Conn.: Keats Publishing, 1980.

[2] Wallach, J. D. and Lan, Ma. *Rare Earths*. Bonita, CA: Double Happiness Publishing, 1966.

Chapter 6. What Vitamins Do What To Which Parts?

[1] Rising Tide Nutrition News, Portsmouth, NH

Chapter 7. How Amino Acids Make Your Child Smarter

[1] Sahley, Billie. *Healing With Amino Acids,* San Antonio, Texas: Pain and Stress Center Publications,1995.

[2,3] Sahley, Billie. *The Anxiety Epidemic*. San Antonio, Texas: Watercrest Press, 1986. Also, *The Natural Way to Control Hyperactivity*. San Antonio, Texas: Pain and Stress Center Publications,1994.

Membership Information/Order Forms

Information and product order forms are also available at http://www.howtolearn.com or http://www.discoveries.org.

Telephone Orders: Call 1 (707) 837-8180 Visa and Mastercard orders only. FAX Orders: 1 (707) 837-9190.
Postal Orders: The Center for New Discoveries In Learning, P.O. Box 1019, Windsor, CA 95492-1019. Call for international shipping rates.

Join The Center for New Discoveries in Learning **and receive FREE educational products valued at over $100.00! All our products are fully guaranteed.**

With your *Red Star* membership you receive:

1. **What's Food Got To Do With It?** (Book)
2. **Super Speller Strategy Video.** Guarantees spelling success.
3. **12 issues of School Smart Kids Newsletter -** 1 new learning strategy each month covering all subject areas, plus reviews on the latest books, tapes and information on successful learning tips for your child.
4. **Baroque Music Tape -** Guaranteed to speed up learning time and increase memory.

Total value = $106.00. Your Membership price is $49.95.

You may also choose our *Gold Star Membership* **for $119.95** and receive all of the above, plus, your choice of **The Gift of Dyslexia,** an 8 hour dyslexia correction course by Ron Davis, author of *The Gift of Dyslexia;* or **Super Teaching Strategies,** an 8 hour video course by Pat Wyman, M.A., covering reading comprehension, math facts, vocabulary, faster reading strategies, study skills and mind-mapping techniques in all subject areas. These tape sets sell separately for $159.00 in catalogs throughout the United States.

Product Descriptions

The Gift of Dyslexia Videos (4 two - hour tapes) by author Ron Davis. These tapes are the video version of *The Gift of Dyslexia* Book and give step by step directions for correcting dyslexia. Don't let your child suffer another day with difficulty in reading - correct it today!

Super Teaching Strategies Videos contain all the successful learning strategies your child will ever need to complete success in school. Teach your child "how to learn" for a lifetime with these 4 two hour videos. Parents and teachers alike have used the Super Teaching Strategies videos to raise their children's' grades to A's and B's in reading, vocabulary, math facts, study skills, science, etc. Documented results show that CTBS scores (national reading, language and math testing) have been raised over 15 percentile points after using the strategies on these videos.

School Smart Kids Newsletter is published monthly and has a subscription price of $49.95. The subscription includes 12 issues of the newsletter with a new learning success strategy each month, as well as information on the latest books and tapes for your child's educational success. Health and wellness tips are also included. This is included in a Red or Gold Star Membership.

Super Speller Strategy Video is a 30 minute video guaranteed to raise your child's spelling grades to A's and B's. Audience is grades 1-8. This video has been proven to raise spelling grades with over 40,000 students.

I'm Smart, I Taught Myself the Times Tables by Joy Ridenour.

Available in both English and Spanish, this is a wonderful 3 ring binder full of reproducible sheets and audio tapes for children learning their times tables.

To Strengthen Visual Skills - A+ Vision
A+ Vision contains hundreds of fun and easy to do eye exercises to help your child read more efficiently and smoothly. The entire book is reproducible.

Smart Foods, Smart Kids - Meal Planner for Parents and Kids

Plan all your meals for maximum learning success. Includes recipes, food rotation, nutritional information and specific products to buy for your child.

Note to teachers
Our video courses, *Super Teaching Strategies* and *The Gift of Dyslexia,* may be taken for 4.5 quarter or 3 semester academic or continuing education units. Please call us for more information at 1 (707) 837-8180.

Order Form

Quantity		Total

Red Star Membership (book, video, newsletters, audio tape)	$ 49.95	
Gold Star Membership (includes above plus one of the video sets)	$ 119.95	
The Gift of Dyslexia Videos		
Super Teaching Strategies Videos		
What's Food Got To Do With It? Book	$ 12.95	
School Smart Kids Newsletter 12 issues	$ 49.95	
Baroque Music Tape	$ 12.95	
I'm Smart, I Taught Myself the Times Tables	$ 59.95	
A+ Vision	$ 29.95	
Smart Foods, Smart Kids - Meal Planner	$ 5.95	
Add $4.00 shipping/handling to each product.		
Add $7.50 shipping to either of the memberships.		
CA residents must add 7.5% sales tax.		
Total of your order	$	

Name _____

Address_____

City, State, Zip _____

Telephone Number

(_____)_____

E-Mail Address _____

Credit Card Number with Exp. Date (Visa or Mastercard Only)

_____Exp._____

Check Enclosed - Circle One: Yes No   Mail or fax your order to: The Center for New Discoveries in Learning, P.O. Box 1019, Windsor, CA 95492-1019. Telephone: 1 (707) 837-8180. FAX 1 (707) 837-9190.

Products may also be ordered from the website at http://www.discoveries.org

Send for your Free Copy of *School Smart Kids* Newsletter

School Smart Kids newsletter contains a new learning success strategy each month, as well as information on the latest books and tapes for your child's educational success. Breakthrough learning techniques, health and wellness tips are also included.

Name _____

Address _____

City, State, Zip
_____

Telephone Number
(_____)_____

FAX Number (_____) _____

E-Mail Address _____

Mail or fax your order to: The Center for New Discoveries in Learning, P.O. Box 1019, Windsor, CA 95492-1019.
Please include a self-addressed stamped envelope.

FAX 707 837-9190. Telephone: 1 (707) 837-8180.

Newsletter is also available on our website at:
http://www.howtolearn.com